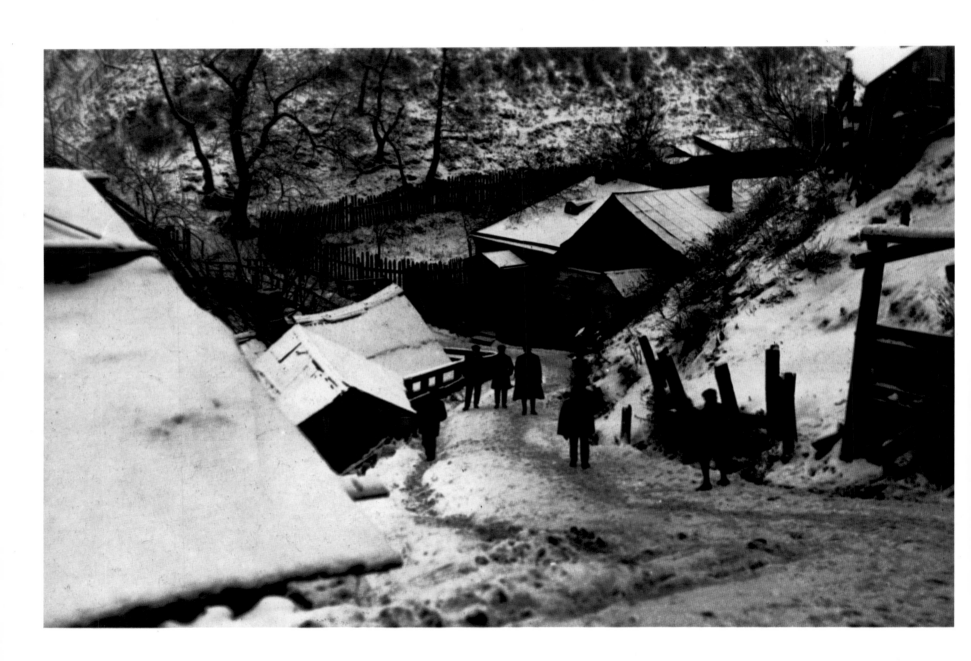

POYLN

Jewish Life in the Old Country

ALTER KACYZNE

Edited by Marek Web

Published in conjunction with
YIVO Institute for Jewish Research,
and with the help of Sulamita Kacyzne-Reale

AN OWL BOOK · HENRY HOLT AND COMPANY · NEW YORK

Henry Holt and Company, LLC
Publishers since 1866
115 West 18th Street
New York, New York 10011

Henry Holt® is a registered trademark of
Henry Holt and Company, LLC.

Grateful acknowledgment is made to The Forward Association, Inc.,
for its generous assistance in publishing this volume.

Distributed in Canada by H. B. Fenn and Company Ltd.

Library of Congress Cataloging-in-Publication Data
Kacyzne, Alter, 1885–1941.
Poyln: Jewish life in the old country—1st ed.
      p.   cm.
Contains a reproduction of photographs taken by Alter Kacyzne
portraying pre-World War II Polish Jewish communities.
ISBN 0-8050-6829-5
      1. Jews—Poland—Pictorial works. 2. Poland—Pictorial works.
      I. Title
DS135.P6K323   1999   99-14178
943.8'004924—dc21   CIP

Henry Holt books are available for special promotions and
premiums. For details contact: Director, Special Markets.

First published in the United States in 1999 by
Metropolitan Books/Henry Holt and Company.

Designed by Lucy Albanese

Frontispiece: Grodno (Białystok province), 1927

Printed in the United States of America
1   3   5   7   9   10   8   6   4   2

CONTENTS

Dos lebn shprotst, dos lebn blit, farblit
A velt fargeyt, a velt banayt di koykhes,
Un tsankt a mentsh, farblaybt nokh im zayn lid
A shpliter gold in shtoybikn paroykhes

Life buds, it blossoms and fades,
A world expires and then renews its strength,
And though a person flickers, his song remains—
In the dusty Torah curtain, a trace of gold.

ALTER KACYZNE

Translation: Jeffrey Shandler

ACKNOWLEDGMENTS

THE IDEA OF AN ALBUM devoted to the photography of Alter Kacyzne had the support of many people who worked enthusiastically to bring the project to fruition. Sulamita Kacyzne-Reale, Alter Kacyzne's daughter, spared no time or effort to keep YIVO's interest in the project alive. Just as she worked tirelessly to preserve and publish her father's literary output, Mrs. Kacyzne-Reale never ceased encouraging YIVO to make his photographic masterworks available in a single volume. Thus the appearance of this book in print is largely the result of her efforts on behalf of Alter Kacyzne and his creative legacy, although, sadly, she passed away a few months prior to publication and so did not see the fruit of her labors. We are also grateful to Mrs. Kacyzne-Reale, and to Samuel Norich and Harold Ostroff of The Forward Association, Inc., for enabling YIVO freely to make use of Kacyzne's photographic archive.

Much of the credit for this album goes to my colleagues at YIVO. The late Dr. Lucjan Dobroszycki broached the subject of producing a Kacyzne album as early as 1979. Roberta Newman, former curator of photographic collections at the YIVO Archives, worked diligently on organizing the Kacyzne photographs and planning for their publication. Krysia Fisher, the current photo curator, helped with evaluating and assembling the photographs for this volume. Andrea Raab Sherman, in her former capacity as YIVO's director of publications, initiated the most recent revival of this project at YIVO and expertly oversaw the publication's progress. Dr. Lisa Epstein, director of research, read the text and offered valuable suggestions. YIVO board member Max Gitter graciously offered the assistance of his colleagues, Gidon Caine, Lynn Bayard, and Olivier Sultan at Paul, Weiss, Rifkind, Wharton & Garrison, who generously gave of their time and advice on legal matters. Kathleen Anderson of Scovil, Chichak, Galen Literary Agency represented the project with tremendous enthusiasm and expertise, and secured for the book its ideal home.

My very special thanks go to Sara Bershtel and Riva Hocherman of Metropolitan Books. Over the years Sara Bershtel has been a steadfast believer in the project, carrying her resolve to make it happen until she found the means to publish the book under the imprint of Metropolitan Books. Riva Hocherman has been wonderful as the album's editor. Her warmth, intelligence, and commitment made our collaboration a worthwhile experience.

Lastly, I wish to dedicate my work on this book to the memory of my parents, Shmuel and Miriam Web, true Jews from the land of Poyln.

MAREK WEB

INTRODUCTION

In Alter Kacyzne's lifetime, Poland was home to 3.1 million Jews, almost all of whom spoke Yiddish. Indeed, in a 1931 census 80 percent of Polish Jews declared Yiddish their mother tongue. And to them Poland was Poyln, Warsaw was Varshe, Kráków was Kroke; the picturesque town of Kazimierz on the river Vistula was Kuzmir oyf der Vaysl; and the little hamlet Zdzięcioł—for no apparent reason—was known as Zhetl. One story has it that when a Viennese Jew asked a Galician Jew the name of the city their train was passing through, the *galitsyaner* said, "The gentiles say Rzeszów, but the whole world calls it Rayshe."

Alter Kacyzne belonged to that world. He was born in Wilno (then part of the Russian Empire and now Vilnius, in Lithuania), but Warsaw, or rather Varshe, was his true home. As a writer he made important contributions to Yiddish literature, as a dramatist to the Yiddish stage. It is as a photographer, however, that he gave his greatest gift to the Jews of Poyln, memorializing his people in a series of brilliant and powerful portraits that restore to us the poignancy, warmth, and spirit of Poland's once-vital Jewish world.

Alter-Sholem Kacyzne was born on May 31, 1885, to a family of Wilno laborers. His grandfather was a blacksmith; his father, Shmuel-Hirsh, a bricklayer; his mother a seamstress. The family lived in perpetual poverty. For a few years Kacyzne attended a traditional *kheyder*, then a Russian Jewish elementary school, and that was the sum of his formal education. He was, however, an avid reader, a self-taught man, and over time he became fluent in Yiddish, Hebrew, Russian, Polish, German, and French.

At fourteen, Kacyzne's life changed dramatically: First his father died; then he was sent to distant Ekaterinoslav in southern Ukraine, where he became a photographer's apprentice. For eleven years Kacyzne worked in a storefront "atelier," as the shop would have been called. He must have found an inspired teacher, someone who taught him more than just technical skills, for somewhere along the line the talented and impressionable young apprentice acquired the expertise that turned him from a craftsman into an artist.

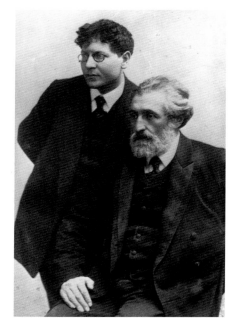

Alter Kacyzne and S. Ansky, Warsaw, 1919

Ekaterinoslav was to prove important in more ways than one. It was here that Kacyzne began to write, but Ekaterinoslav was not Poyln, and Russian, not Yiddish, was the preferred language. Enthusiastically, Kacyzne embraced the language of Pushkin and Tolstoy and began writing Russian poetry of his own, eventually finding the courage to send some of his work to S. Ansky, the renowned writer and editor of the Russian periodical *Yevreyskii mir* (The Jewish World). In 1909 Ansky published two of Kacyzne's pieces and wrote him a warm and encouraging letter. About that time Kacyzne married Khana Khachanov, the daughter of a local Jewish family. Altogether he was well on his way to fitting into the Russian Jewish mold.

At that point, however, Kacyzne made a discovery that was to alter the direction of his life. He stumbled across the stories of Isaac Leib Peretz, one of the founders of modern Yiddish literature. A leading figure in the Jewish cultural renaissance at the turn of the century, Peretz had been in large measure responsible for making Warsaw the center of Yiddish culture. Throngs of young writers flocked to his Warsaw home, inspired by his vision of the Yiddish language's seminal role in Jewish life, by his belief that Yiddish writers had the mission of creating a modern national literature, by his activist social philosophy, by his fascination with Jewish folklore and the Hasidic tradition, above all by his ability to blend all these elements into a cohesive program.

Enthralled by Peretz's writings, Kacyzne resolved to move to Warsaw, and in 1910 he and his young wife left Ekaterinoslav. Kacyzne became Peretz's most devoted disciple; his adulation was legendary. What was good for Peretz was law for Kacyzne. "There was a portrait of Peretz hanging in Kacyzne's apartment," wrote the poet Kadia Molodowsky, "and I always had the impression that Kacyzne wouldn't do a thing without first talking it over with Peretz's likeness." Indeed, until 1915, when Peretz died, Kacyzne was content to live in his mentor's shadow, not even trying to publish his own work. "I was learning how to write from Peretz, working on it very methodically. What was the method? I kept writing and he kept erasing. This went on for more than two years, week after week."[1]

IN 1918 KACYZNE PUBLISHED his first work in Yiddish; he was thirty-three years old. Over the next twenty-five years he produced a sizable body of writings that included poetry, plays, short stories, a novel, film scripts, cultural and social essays, travel journals, and news articles. His style was eclectic, moving from the enigmatic symbolism of his first poem, "Der gayst der meylekh" (The Soul of the King), to the artful simplicity of the folkloristic *Baladn un groteskn* (Ballads and Grotesques, 1936); from the stylized short stories *Arabeskn* (1922), written in the vein of the Song of Songs and *The Arabian Nights*, to the realistic novel *Shtarke un shvakhe* (The Strong and the Weak, 1930), a vast panorama of Polish Jewish life set during World War I. As a dramatist Kacyzne expanded the Yiddish theater's repertoire with his four historical plays—*Dukus* (The Duke, 1925), the Shakespearean *Hurdus* (Herod, 1926), *Dem yidns opere* (The Jew's Opera, 1937), and *Shvartsbard* (1937)—which were dominated by themes of Jewish destiny and anti-Jewish persecution.

Kacyzne's activities touched on every major Yiddish cultural enterprise. He was founder, editor, and columnist for several important publications; a board member of the Yiddish Writers and Journalists Association, commonly known as the Literatn-farayn; chairman of the Yiddish PEN Club; executor and editor of the literary estates of Peretz and Ansky. He supervised the publication of Ansky's collected works, completing Ansky's unfinished play *Tog un nakht* (Day and Night). He had close ties to Di Khalyastre (The Gang), a group of young modernist Yiddish writers that took its name from the journal founded by the poet Peretz Markish; others in the group included Israel Joshua Singer, the future bard of Hebrew poetry Uri Zvi Greenberg, and the poet Melekh Ravitch; Marc Chagall contributed illustrations. In addition to literary production, Kacyzne collaborated with the leading Yiddish theater groups of the day and pioneering Yiddish film producers. He traveled widely as a press photographer and journalist.

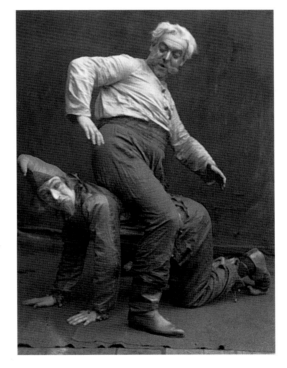

Warsaw actor Abraham Morewski in a performance of *The Duke*, 1925

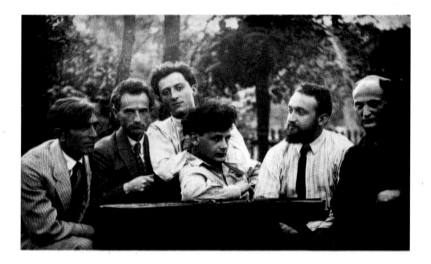

Di Khalyastre at the Świder summer house. *From left:* Mendl Elkin, Peretz Hirschbein, Uri Zvi Greenberg, Peretz Markish, Melekh Ravitch, Israel Joshua Singer

Known for his left-wing sympathies, he became the editor of the thinly disguised Communist Yiddish daily *Der Fraynd* (The Friend) in 1935, a time when such a step was certain to bring state prosecution. From 1937 to 1939 Kacyzne published a sixteen-page biweekly called *Mayn redndiker film* (My Talking Film), which was filled exclusively with his own literary writings and political commentary. Kacyzne was a veritable cultural institution, inextricably bound to Jewish Warsaw.

The Kacyznes lived in the very heart of their community. Their first home was on Świętojerska Street, in a small but well-kept apartment at the center of Jewish Warsaw. When a daughter, Sulamita, was born in 1925, Alter and Khana moved to a much larger place on Nowolipie, across the street from the popular Socialist Yiddish daily *Folkstsaytung*. Around 1920 Kacyzne had bought a summer house in Świder, a resort town some twenty miles from Warsaw. Famous for its long, sandy stretches, pine trees, and pine-scented air—considered good for weak lungs—the area came to life in the summer with thousands of Jewish vacationers, children attending camps, and consumptives crowding into the sanatoriums. Świder's shallow, gentle stream, called, naturally, the Świder, was a beloved spot for sunbathing and swimming. Kacyzne made his house available for summer rentals and in a short time it became a preferred retreat for writers, mostly Kacyzne's colleagues, who loudly complained of the rent their friend was charging them. The place had the air of a bohemian enclave and the roster of guests was truly impressive. Of course, the entire Khalyastre used to stay there, and the dashing Peretz Markish reigned supreme for several summers. One day Israel Joshua Singer's younger brother came from provincial Stary Dzików for a visit; many years later Isaac Bashevis

Singer recorded his impressions of Kacyzne's house: "What a change from Stary Dzików! Here I'm surrounded by literature, by knowledge, by poetry. Any minute the train may bring a Markish, a Ravitch, an Uri Zvi Greenberg. Who hasn't shown up? They say that the writer Peretz Hirschbein is here from America with his wife, Esther Shumiatcher, who also writes poetry. Soon Opatoshu will come, Dr. Zhitlowsky, maybe Abraham Reisen."[2]

THOUGH LITTLE IS KNOWN about Kacyzne's early years in Warsaw, it seems clear that he continued working as a photographer. He opened a studio on Długa Street, close to where he lived, specializing in individual portraits, weddings, bar mitzvahs, confirmations, and other social occasions. Around 1926 the studio moved a few blocks to Bielańska Street, and finally in 1930 Kacyzne decided to transfer the business out of the Jewish neighborhood altogether, to Wileńska Street in the borough of Praga on the other side of the Vistula. There it remained until the Kacyznes fled Warsaw in September 1939.

Kacyzne's studio flourished. It became something of a vogue among Warsaw's Jews to be photographed by him; a young man who wanted to compliment his date would tell her she looked "like a Kacyzne picture." Eventually, Kacyzne was able to hire assistants, one of whom was Israel Joshua Singer, a photographic retoucher long before he became the best-selling author of the novels *Yoshe Kalb*, *The Brothers Ashkenazi*, and *The Family Carnovsky*. In fact, Kacyzne's studio provided the setting for Singer's very first short story, "In der fintsternish" (In the Darkness).[3] The studio he describes is enviable: a large salon with a fireplace, plenty of daylight streaming through the large glass windows, and a fully stocked darkroom.

It is tantalizing to think of the monumental photographic archive Kacyzne surely amassed during his lifetime. Within the studio and around Warsaw, he photographed a vast range of people, from the poor to the wealthy, the ordinary to the

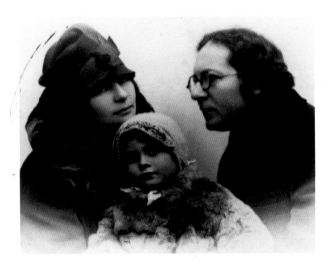

Khana, Sulamita, and Alter Kacyzne, Warsaw, ca. 1930

famous. He took his camera to the theater, to readings, to political meetings, and often he went on photographic expeditions. The many writers, journalists, actors, and other celebrities who visited the Świder retreat found themselves the subjects of Kacyzne portraits. No doubt his archive would have formed one of our great historical records had it survived the Holocaust. None of it did, though, not a shred. Kacyzne's papers, manuscripts, family documents, and priceless photographs—everything—perished in the Nazi occupation.

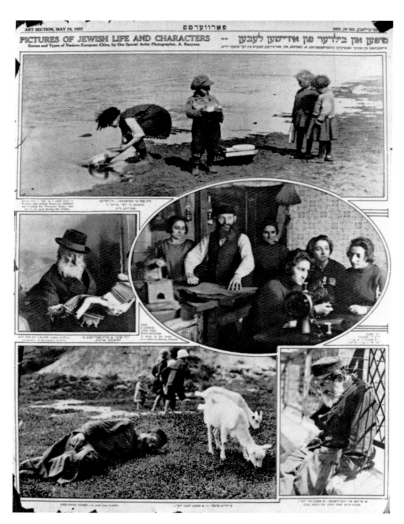

"Our Special Artist Photographer," the *Forverts*, May 24, 1925

Yet Alter Kacyzne's chronicle of Jewish life in Poland has not been completely obliterated. A small but all-important fraction of his photographs survived, some seven hundred prints in all, sent by Kacyzne to the United States in the 1920s. Preserved to this day in the archives of the YIVO Institute for Jewish Research in New York, they are the sole remnant of Kacyzne's artistry.

The story of these photographs began with a commission in 1921, when Kacyzne was asked by the Hebrew Immigrant Aid Society (HIAS) in New York to illustrate the plight of Jews seeking to leave Poland. At the time the society's regional office in Warsaw was virtually besieged by thousands of Jews desperate to secure immigration papers to the United States and Kacyzne recorded their hopes and fears in a remarkable series of photographs. Shortly after Kacyzne completed this assignment, Abraham Cahan, editor in chief of the New York Yiddish newspaper the *Forverts*, or the *Jewish Daily Forward*, invited him to work for the paper. His job was to document images of Jewish life in the "old country" for the benefit of *Forverts* readers, who were mostly of immigrant stock. Thus Kacyzne found himself working for a mighty mass-circulation daily in America, a dream job for a Yiddish writer in inflation-ridden, war-ravaged Poland.

The terms of the commission were rather vague. "Abraham Cahan has hired me to be the photo correspondent for the *Forverts*," Kacyzne explained in 1925 to Baruch Vladeck, the paper's business manager.[4] "My task is to cover all the places in Poland that may be of interest to the reader in America. Comrade Cahan thought this program would take me two years to complete." In fact, Kacyzne spent a decade of his life toiling for the *Forverts*, or more specifically for its illustrated Sunday supplement, "The Art Section." This strikingly handsome rotogravure insert, the first of its kind in the Yiddish press, was filled with art reproductions, news about celebrities, and "picture contributions from our readers and correspondents." Kacyzne was the supplement's star photographer and his images fulfilled an important function: They evoked nostalgia and longing but at the same time made clear to former immigrants just how much they had gained by leaving the shtetl once and for all and embracing their new lives in America.

Kacyzne worked hard to meet the constant demand for new material. Every few weeks he packed up his equipment and set out for the countryside in search of themes, scenes, and types. In his letters to Cahan, Kacyzne often complained that his work was subject to the whims of the weather, that he would get stuck in remote towns for days without taking a single picture, that he had personally to finance the whole operation because the *Forverts* was three or four or six months late with his payments. On one occasion, when Cahan questioned an expense of fifty dollars, Kacyzne exploded:

> If you think being tossed about along these broken old Polish back roads is such a great pleasure, you're much mistaken. I do this because I have to look for more material. If I just sat around in Warsaw I'd have no new stuff for you. You seem to be asking me how I get around. Well, if I send you photographs from Galicia or Volhynia, it's because I'm there on a lecture tour—I do also happen to be a writer, Comrade Cahan. And while I'm there, I spend a day taking pictures for the *Forverts*. The expenses for these long trips are

covered by my lectures, not by the *Forverts*. It wouldn't cost you any less if I stayed closer to Warsaw. So all I'm charging you for are these paltry expenses. I simply can't get the same scenes and faces in Warsaw. The blacksmiths, the spinning women in Żelechów, the *kheyder* boys, and the politicians in Łuków, they're all of photographic and artistic as well as ethnographic value. The *Forverts* now claims all my time and is my only livelihood. I've had to close down my studio. I just can't dance at two weddings at the same time.

Momentary irritations and financial haggling aside, Kacyzne's work for the *Forverts* continued, earning him the substantial monthly sum of $150 and considerable envy among his literary colleagues. "He also works for the *Forverts*. Every few weeks he sends in a couple of photos and for this he gets paid pretty well. They say he's rich," Isaac Bashevis Singer recalled in his memoirs.[5]

The *Forverts* was getting its money's worth too. Kacyzne traveled to scores of cities, towns, hamlets, indeed to the farthest corners of Poland, wherever he sensed the opportunity for interesting material. The YIVO collection of Kacyzne's *Forverts* prints comprises pictures taken in more than 120 localities, from Warsaw to the far-flung countryside. In a clear sign of appreciation, Cahan asked Kacyzne in 1925 to accompany him to Palestine as the official *Forverts* photographer. In later years Kacyzne traveled to Romania, Italy, Spain, and Morocco, all the while sending photographs to New York.

Still, all was not well between Kacyzne and the *Forverts*. While he took much pride in his photographic work, he saw himself principally as a writer and his true goal was to write for the paper. He would send Cahan one idea after another suggesting ways to use him as a writer *and* a photographer:

> I propose you introduce something new in the *Forverts*, a column called "With the *Forverts* Camera" that would include impressions about people, places, and events photographed by the paper. I think your readers who see Kacyzne's pictures in the Sunday edition would also be interested to read Kacyzne's thoughts about his subjects. It would make my work less mechanical. It's a hard thing, dear friend Cahan, to trudge from one shtetl to another and see the same Jews and their women, as if they all came from one family. Even with the best intentions, it's hard to find truly new material.

On another occasion he implored Cahan to send him to the Soviet Union, but Cahan dispatched I. J. Singer, the *Forverts*'s Poland correspondent, instead. As far as Cahan was concerned, Singer was the *Forverts*'s writer in Poland and Kacyzne the photographer. Even more painful for Kacyzne was the fact that Cahan refused to publish any of his other literary efforts. The *Forverts*'s rejection had no impact on Kacyzne's literary career in Poland, where the publisher B. Kleckin and the most important Yiddish journals readily printed his work, but it certainly had a cooling effect on relations between Kacyzne and Cahan. The result was that this author, whose prolific work included much travel writing from foreign countries, never published so much as a paragraph about his journeys through the land of Poyln.

If we are deprived of Kacyzne's writerly impressions, the loss is in some way repaired by the eloquence of the photographs; they reveal much about their creator, about his technical mastery and his uncommon ability to penetrate his subjects' inner world. In a rare account of Kacyzne at work, the theater director Jacob Rotbaum wrote:

> I had the opportunity to observe Kacyzne's technical and artistic method and was especially struck by his concentration while he studied the sitter's features. I was amazed by his patience and tension as he strove to uncover the subject's most essential, most expressive traits, the person's truest characteristics. With the help of spotlights and projectors, Kacyzne was able to reach the depths of the person's psychological self.[6]

Portrait or landscape, gloomy room or busy marketplace, Kacyzne's photographs were enriched not only by the artist's technical expertise—his stylized compositions and subtle contrasts of light and shadow, his striking angles and cinematic effects—but by his special rapport with his subjects, his profound affinity with the people and their world.

KACYZNE'S OEUVRE REPRESENTS a central link in a chain of documentary and artistic images of Jewish Eastern Europe, which began with Michał Greim, a photographer from eastern Galicia who started making collotypes of Galician Jews in the 1860s. Greim's work was continued by S. Ansky's ethnographic expedition, which explored the provinces of Volhynia and Podolia from 1912 to 1914 recording Jewish folkways. Photography of the Jews reached its peak in the inter-war years with the work of Menakhem Kipnis, Alter Kacyzne, and, shortly before World War II, Roman Vishniac, all of whom were prompted by the urge to preserve the imagery of *dis alte heym*, the old world.

Among them, though, Kacyzne's special kinship with the Jews of Poyln speaks with the clearest voice, in a record that is moving, intimate, and memorable in its beauty and authenticity. As the writer Moshe Dluznowsky put it,

> He photographed Jews with all their charm, gestures, and looks, with sorrow and laughter, with suffering and joy. He found his models in the houses and on the streets, in the alleys and behind the workbenches, in the marketplace and in the prayer house. He plucked his subjects from exotic reaches of folklore, cloaked them in the ordinary and the festive, and let them stand with their dreams and their reality, their prayers and their woes, their great burdens and their painterly beauty.[7]

Kacyzne's body of work, however, was by no means all-encompassing. There are no wealthy Jews in his photos and modernizing Jews are not much in evidence either. Rather, it is the shtetl as a historical place and a state of mind that is Kacyzne's real subject. Even his pictures of metropolitan Warsaw and Łódź settle on characters and scenes indistinguishable from those in the remote towns of Husiatyn or Długosiodło. His Jews wear traditional clothes and work at occupations they learned from their fathers and grandfathers. Their living quarters, which often double as workshops, are primitive and overcrowded. Their routes of escape are extremely limited. For the vast majority, escape meant moving to an industrial city and swelling the ranks of the Jewish proletariat. Their dreams of emigration to more hospitable countries were dashed by the exclusionary quotas imposed in America and in Palestine.

Between the world wars, the entire Jewish community in Poland was in a state of social upheaval, economic crisis, and political uncertainty; as a chronicler, Kacyzne chose to show those Polish Jews who were hardest hit. His friend Melekh Ravitch was right when he wrote, "In the end, his atelier fulfilled a tragic historic mission. Kacyzne in his many photographs grasped the tragic, wretched, and holy life of the Jewish people in Poland."

ON THE EVE OF World War II many in Kacyzne's circle, aware of the rise of anti-Semitism and the Nazi victories in neighboring Germany, were determined to leave Poland. Kacyzne resolved to stay on. He had been granted a U.S. visa, which in the end he did not use. He could not bring himself to leave behind all that was meaningful to him and become an immigrant, physically and culturally.

In September 1939, as the Nazis took the Polish capital, the Kacyznes fled Warsaw and found refuge in Lwów in eastern Poland, which was then under Soviet occupation. Kacyzne worked as an editor of Yiddish-language broadcasts on Soviet radio and as artistic director of the local Yiddish theater. When the Nazis broke their pact with the Soviets in June 1941 and began their advance toward Lwów, Alter and Khana Kacyzne tried to flee farther east. They were denied a place on the train that carried other evacuees from Lwów to safety inside Soviet territory and resolved to separate: Alter would try to leave Lwów alone—he was certain the Germans were looking for him on account of his work for the Soviet media. Khana and Sulamita stayed behind, hoping as many did that a woman and child would find it easier to stay out of harm's way. Along with thousands of other refugees, Kacyzne began a desperate trek on foot in the direction of Tarnopol. After a grueling five-day march, he reached Tarnopol, but the Nazis had arrived ahead of him. Their Ukrainian collaborators were in the midst of a murderous anti-Jewish pogrom that lasted from July 4 to July 11 and left five thousand Tarnopol Jews dead. On July 7 Kacyzne was among a group of Jews marched to the Jewish cemetery,

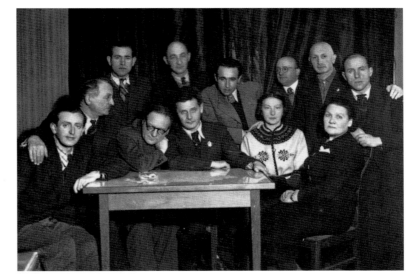

Jewish writers in Lwów, 1941. Alter Kacyzne is sitting at the table, on the left, leaning against Peretz Markish. This is the last known photograph of Kacyzne.

already piled high with corpses. The prisoners endured long hours of unspeakable torture and beatings until they too succumbed one after another. Lying on the ground half-conscious, Alter Kacyzne was discovered to be still breathing. The Ukrainian who found him beat him with a stick and did not stop until he was satisfied that the body on the ground would not move again.

While millions perished without a trace, Alter Kacyzne's terrible death was recorded in the minutest detail. A young Yiddish poet, Nakhman Blitz, was also taken to the Tarnopol cemetery that dreadful July day. Lying only a short distance from the spot where Kacyzne was massacred, Blitz committed the murder to memory. He was one of the few who survived the terror and he crept back to the city when night finally fell. He lived to return to liberated Warsaw in 1945 and published a harrowing account of Alter Kacyzne's last hours in one of the first issues of *Dos naye lebn* (The New Life), a Yiddish daily. Blitz's account was among the earliest Holocaust testimonies to appear in print after the fall of the Nazis.[8]

Alter Kacyzne's wife, Khana, perished in the German death camp in Belzec. His daughter, Sulamita, survived the war disguised as a gentile. In 1946 she married the Italian ambassador to Poland, Eugenio Reale, and moved to Italy, where she lived until her death in 1999. Sulamita Kacyzne-Reale devoted much of her life to preserving her father's literary and artistic legacy.

THE PHOTOGRAPHS REPRODUCED in this volume have been chosen from among the seven hundred prints that make up the Alter Kacyzne Collection in the YIVO Archives. The *Forverts* photographs form the bulk of the collection, although Kacyzne's HIAS commission is preserved here as well.

The *Forverts* prints were made from the negatives by Kacyzne himself; he also wrote his own captions in Yiddish, brief and sometimes whimsical. There is a great deal of intimacy in his captions, as if Kacyzne wanted to point out a kinship between his subjects and the *Forverts*'s readers. Though the newspaper's editors regularly changed the captions, making them longer and more chatty, in this book Kacyzne's original captions have been restored. New text has been added only where there is a need for an explanatory note. All such additional text follows Kacyzne's own in brackets. The earlier HIAS prints have come down to us without any identifying description, however; thus captions have been added.

Generally, Kacyzne selected his photographs for the *Forverts* with something of an anthropologist's eye—according to types of people or categories, such as "Youth" or "Old Age." *Poyln*, an overview of his work, has been conceived differently, however, in an attempt to give a more integrated view of the Jewish world Kacyzne knew and recorded. Thus the chapters in this book have been arranged to provide a sense of the flow of life in Poyln, its different aspects and events. The book opens with "Approaching," a chapter devoted to Kacyzne's broad landscapes of the villages and towns he visited, and proceeds through the rhythms of a community, from the beginning of the day to the weekly markets, the working world, domestic and communal life, religious practice, and finally the process of immigration and departure from the old country.

With regard to dates, all the photographs in this book were taken between 1924 and 1929. Kacyzne used to send the prints to the *Forverts* in batches of several dozen, with a cover list. The lists (which are not extant) were probably dated, but not the individual photographs. Still, some do bear the full date written on the reverse, added by the paper's staff at the time of publication; in such cases, the year appears here as part of the caption. The HIAS photographs were all taken in 1921–22; no specific dates have been given.

After the Holocaust Kacyzne's photographs were reproduced frequently in a variety of media, yet the photographer himself remained in the shadows, largely unknown. *Poyln*, devoted exclusively to Alter Kacyzne's work, will, it is hoped, dispel the shadow around the artist and reveal the splendor of his oeuvre.

MAREK WEB

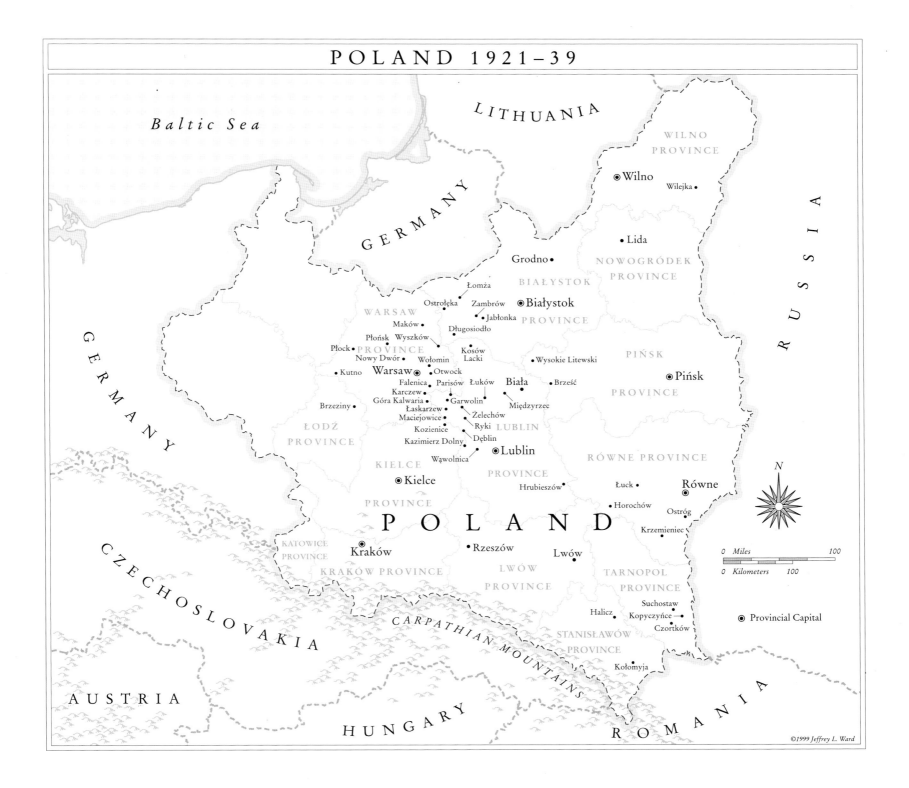

POLAND 1921–39

Baltic Sea

LITHUANIA

GERMANY

RUSSIA

WILNO PROVINCE

⊙ Wilno

• Wilejka

• Lida

Grodno •

NOWOGRÓDEK PROVINCE

BIAŁYSTOK

Łomża •

Ostrołęka •

Zambrów • Jabłonka

⊙ Białystok

PROVINCE

Maków •

Długosiodło •

PIŃSK

Płońsk • Wyszków

Kosów Lacki

• Wysokie Litewski

Płock •

PROVINCE

Nowy Dwór • Wołomin

⊙ Pińsk

• Kutno

Warsaw ⊙ • Otwock

Falenica • Parisów • Łuków

Biała •

• Brześć

PROVINCE

Karczew •

Góra Kalwaria • Garwolin

Międzyrzec

• Brzeziny

Łaskarzew •

Maciejowice • Żelechów

Kozienice • Ryki

LUBLIN

Kazimierz Dolny • Dęblin

ŁÓDŹ PROVINCE

Wąwolnica • ⊙ Lublin

RÓWNE PROVINCE

KIELCE

PROVINCE

⊙ Kielce

Hrubieszów •

• Łuck

Równe ⊙

PROVINCE

• Horochów

• Ostróg

POLAND

• Krzemieniec

0 *Miles* 100

Kraków • Rzeszów

• Lwów

TARNOPOL

0 *Kilometers* 100

KATOWICE PROVINCE

LWÓW

PROVINCE

KRAKÓW PROVINCE

PROVINCE

N

Suchostaw •

CZECHOSLOVAKIA

Halicz • Kopyczyńce •

⊙ Provincial Capital

Czortków •

CARPATHIAN MOUNTAINS

STANISŁAWÓW

PROVINCE

AUSTRIA

Kołomyja •

HUNGARY

ROMANIA

©1999 Jeffrey L. Ward

POYLN

I

APPROACHING

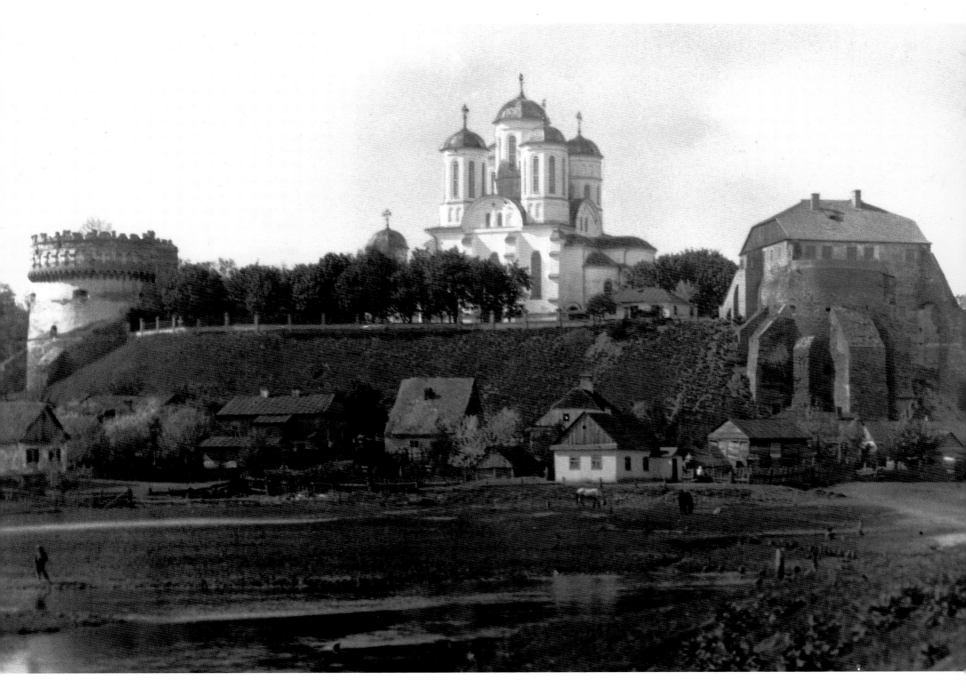

Ostre (Ostróg, Równe province), 1925

The old castle and the synagogue *(right)*, connected by an underground passage

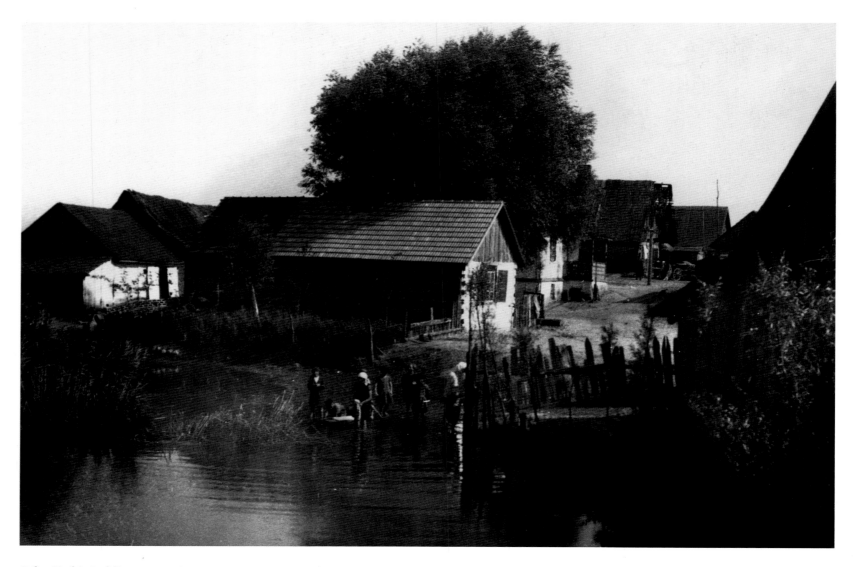

Rike (Ryki, Lublin province)
A little bit of Rike

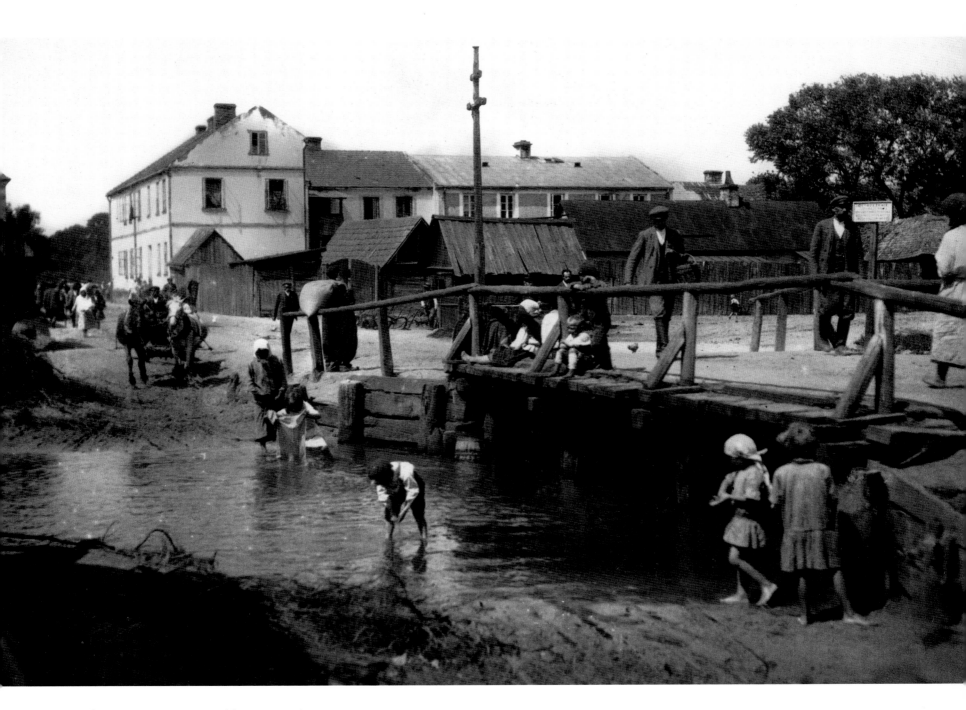

Matshevits (Maciejowice, Lublin province)

At the footbridge

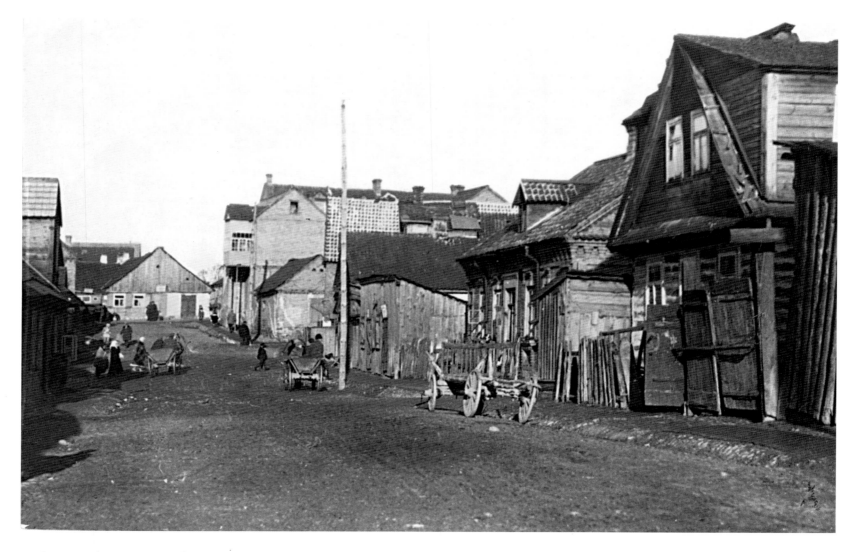

Makeve (Maków Mazowiecki, Warsaw province)

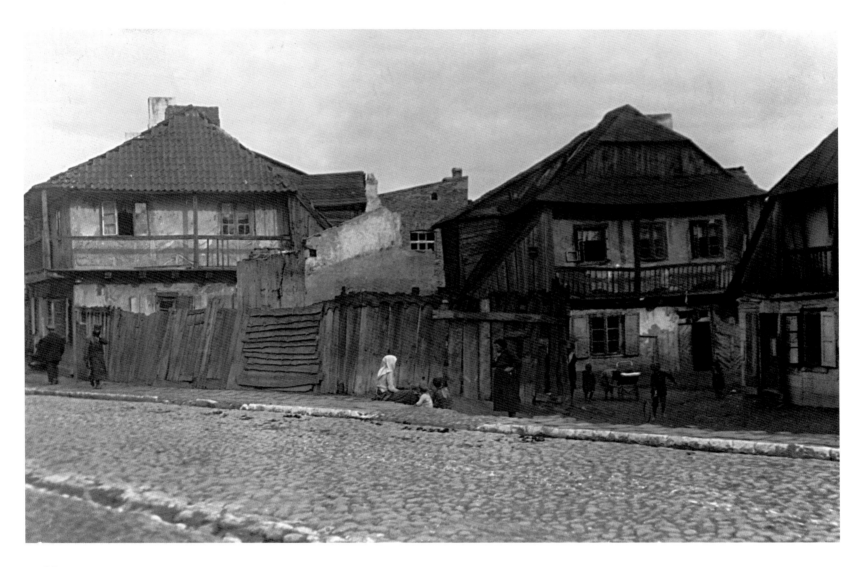

Lublin, 1924

Old Jewish architecture

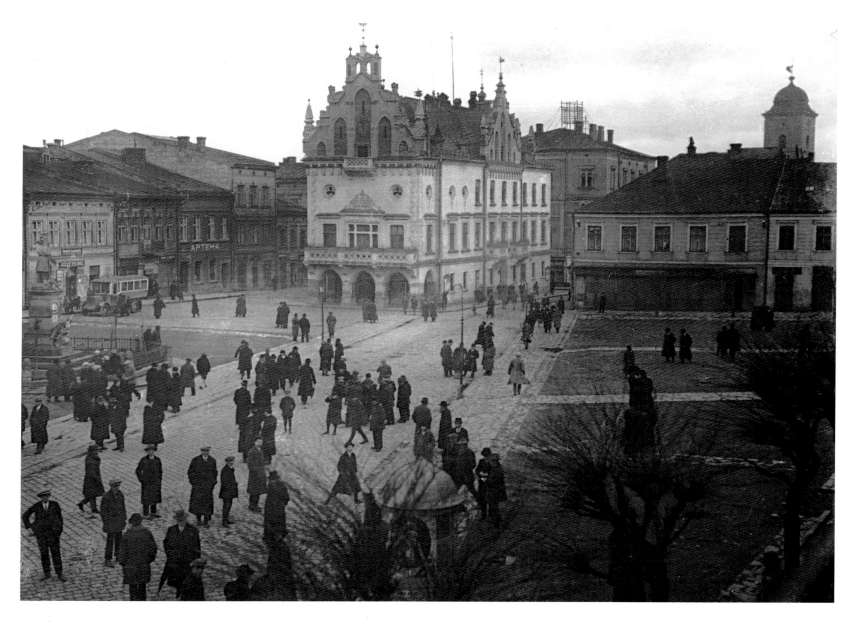

Rayshe (Rzeszów, Lwów province)

A stampede outside the town hall: the dollar is up!

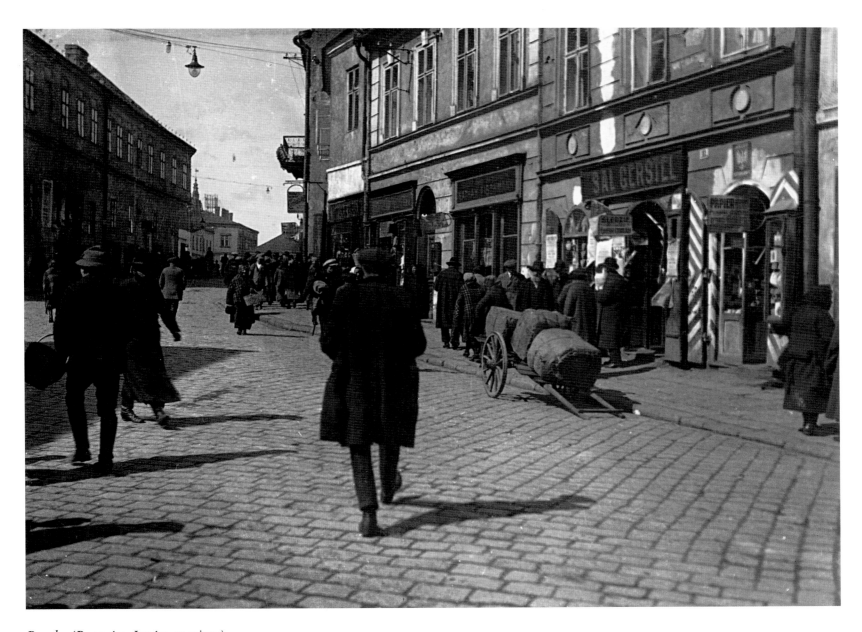

Rayshe (Rzeszów, Lwów province)

In the Jewish neighborhood

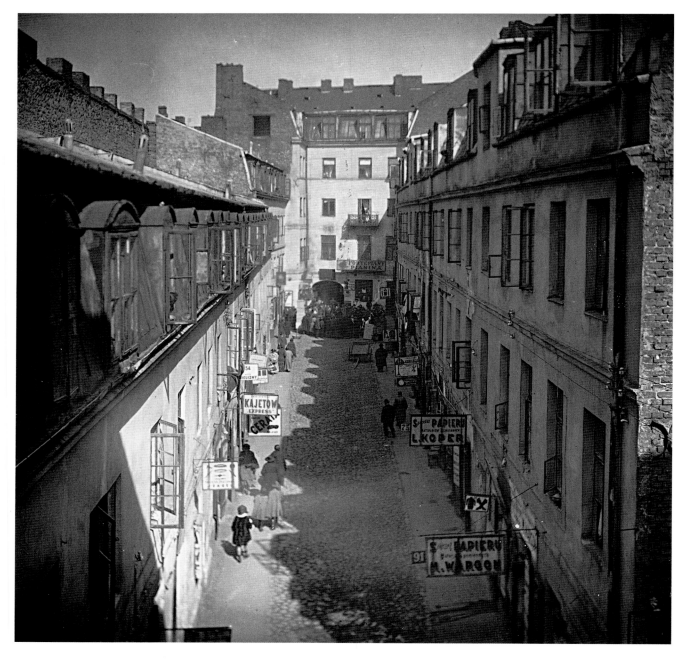

Varshe (Warsaw)

A courtyard on Nalewki Street (known as "the Mlaver's house")

[That is, the landlord came from Mława, a town north of Warsaw.]

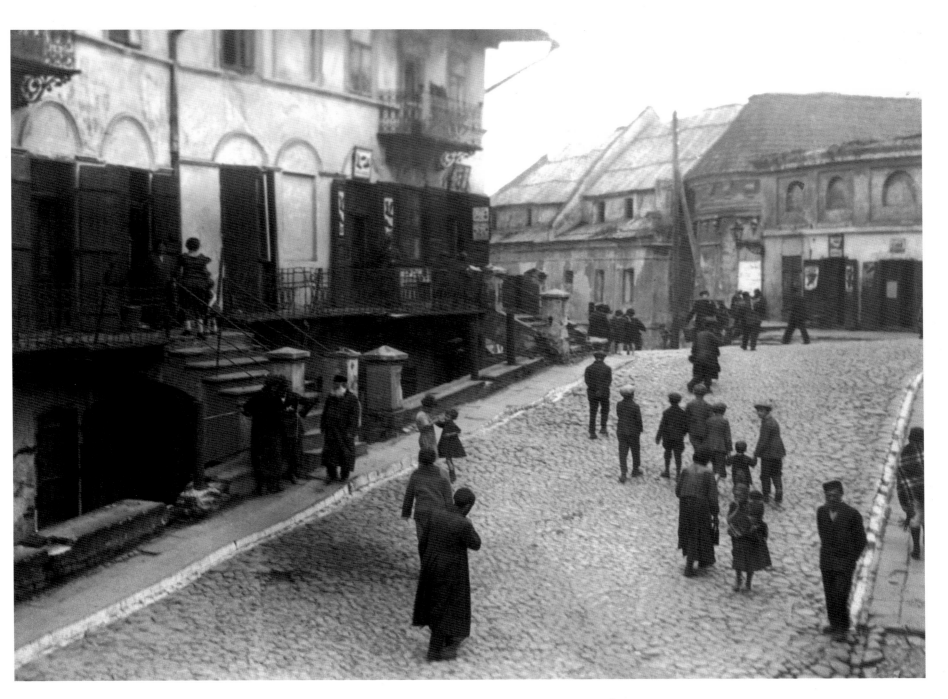

Lublin, 1924

The Jewish bridge (although there is no bridge)

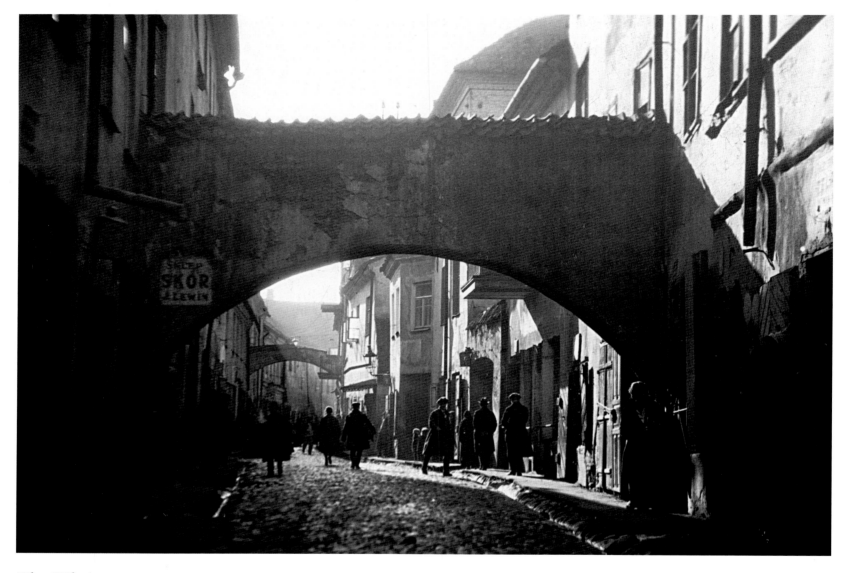

Vilne (Wilno)

Near the *shulhoyf.* Jatkowa Street no. 15, the entrance to the Jewish quarter

[The *shulhoyf,* the courtyard of the Great City Synagogue in Wilno, was in the heart of the Jewish quarter, surrounded by prayer halls, communal offices, a rabbinical library, a ritual bath, and several *kloyzn,* or small synagogues.]

II

STARTING
THE DAY

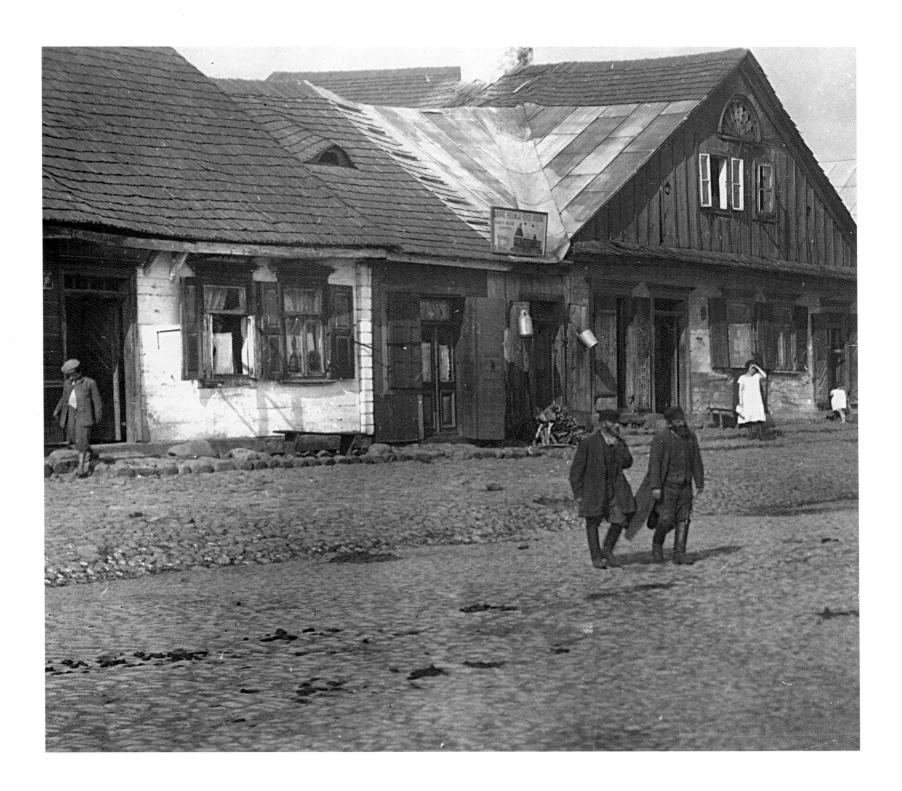

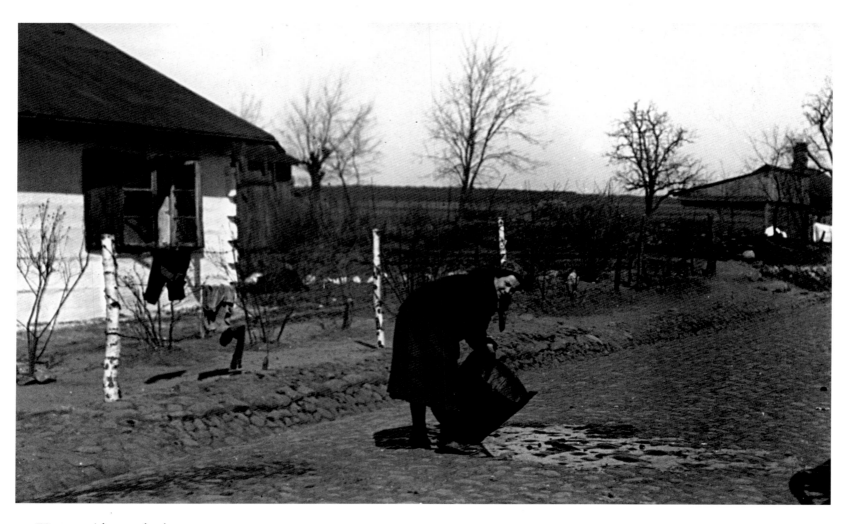

Woman with a washtub

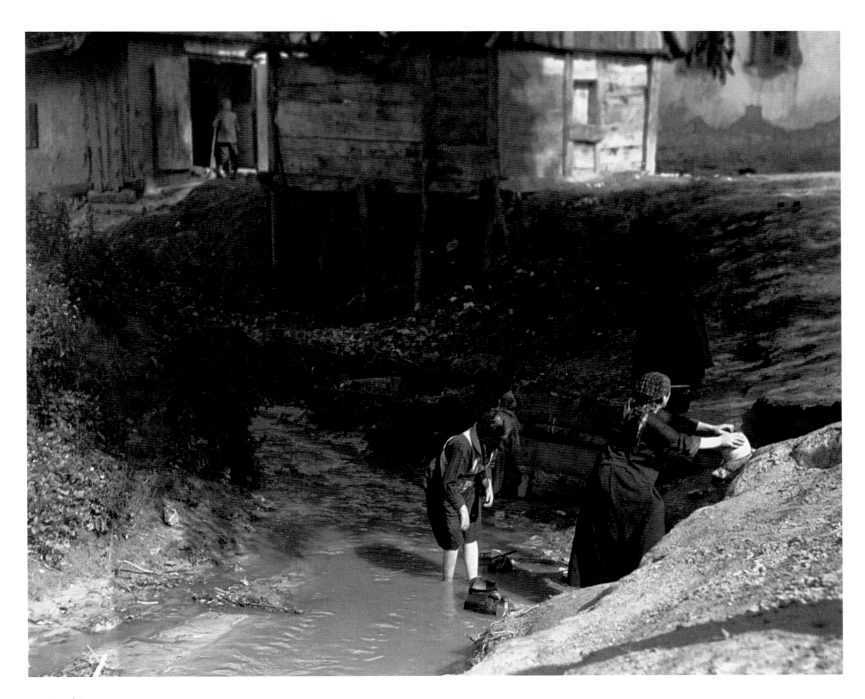

Fetching water

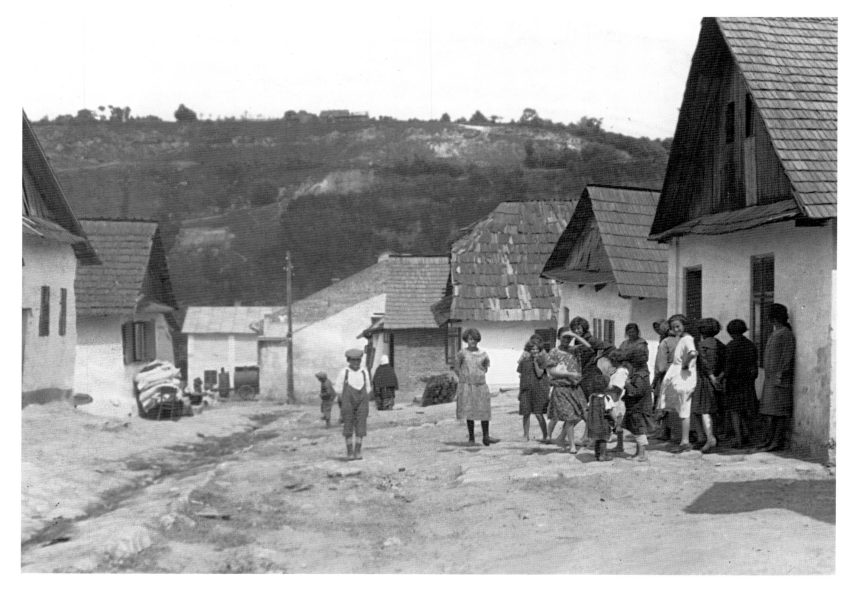

Tshortkev (Czortków, Tarnopol province)
Outside the Weiners' house

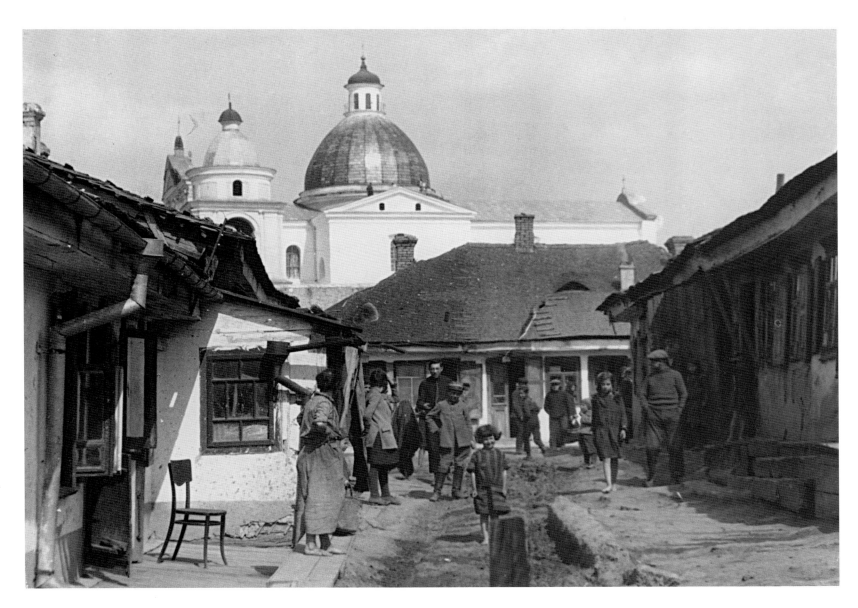

Loytsk (Łuck, Równe province), 1926

A Jewish corner with a touch of the Byzantine

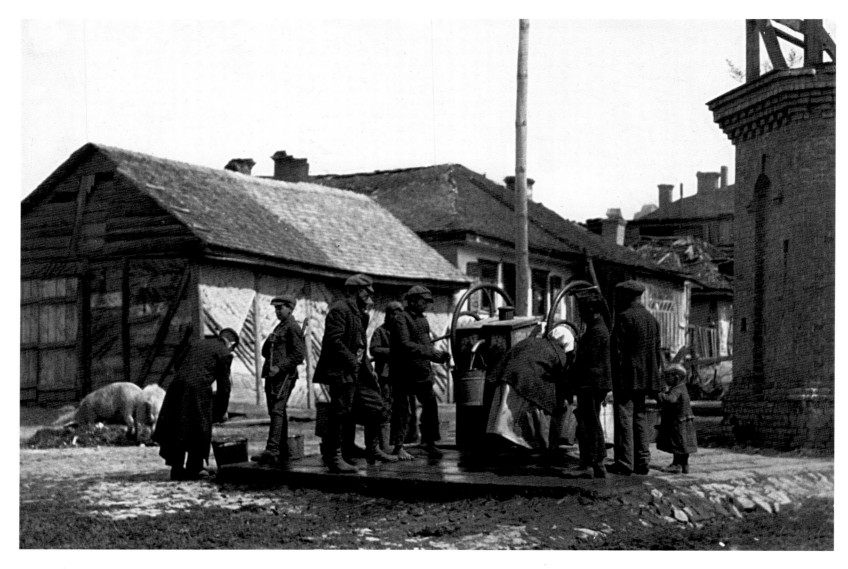

Loytsk (Łuck, Równe province), 1925

At the water pump in the market square

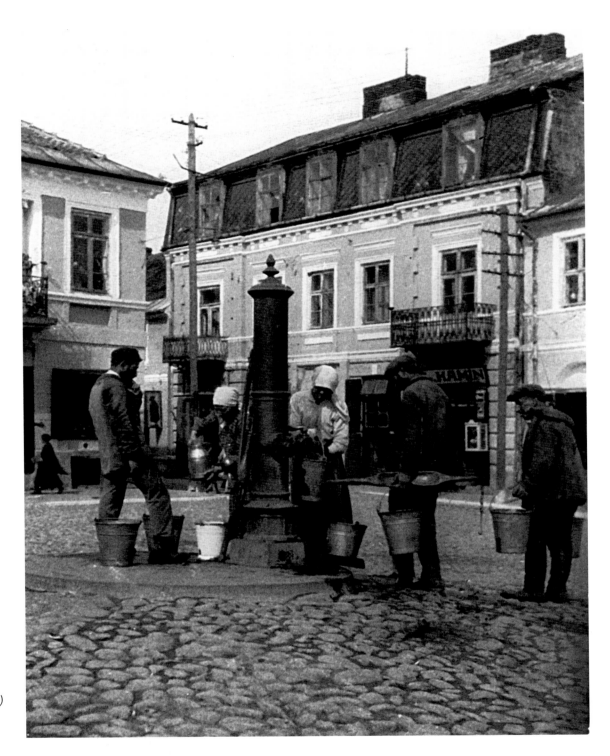

Hlinsk (Glińsko, Lwów province)

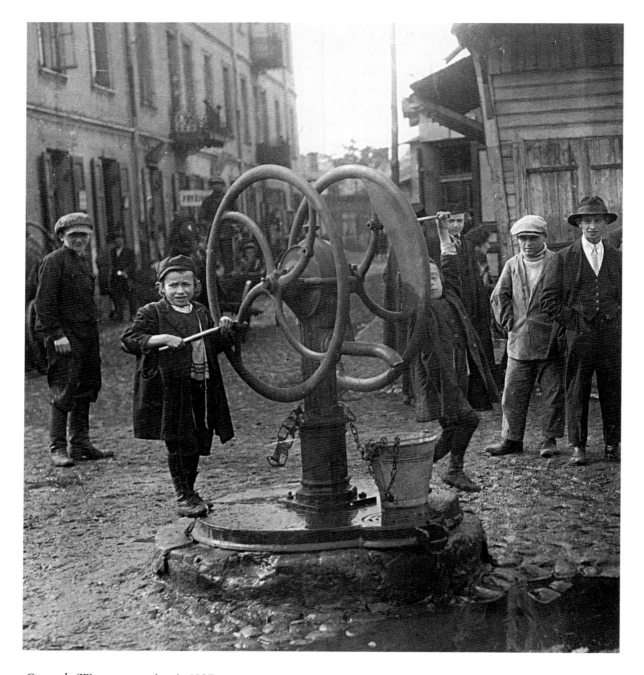

Otwock (Warsaw province), 1927

Otwock's next generation learns how to pour water.

[The phrase *gisn vaser*—to pour water—is also used to describe a windbag.]

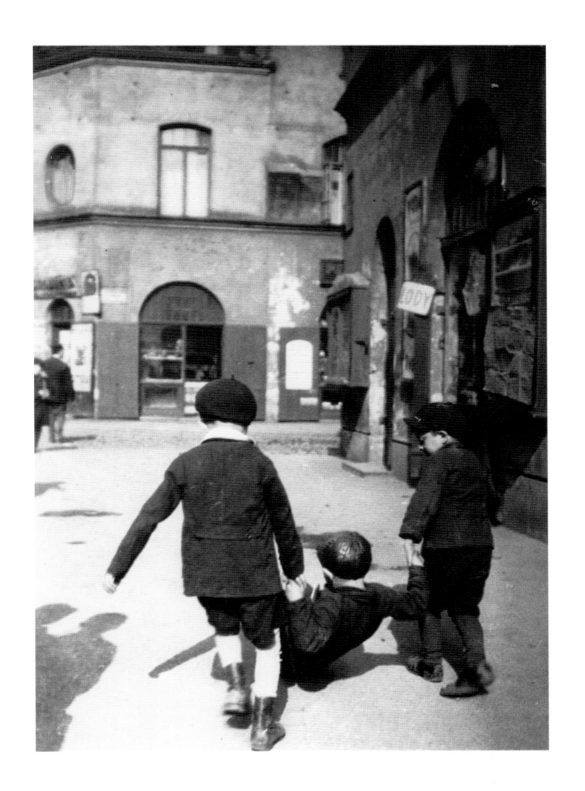

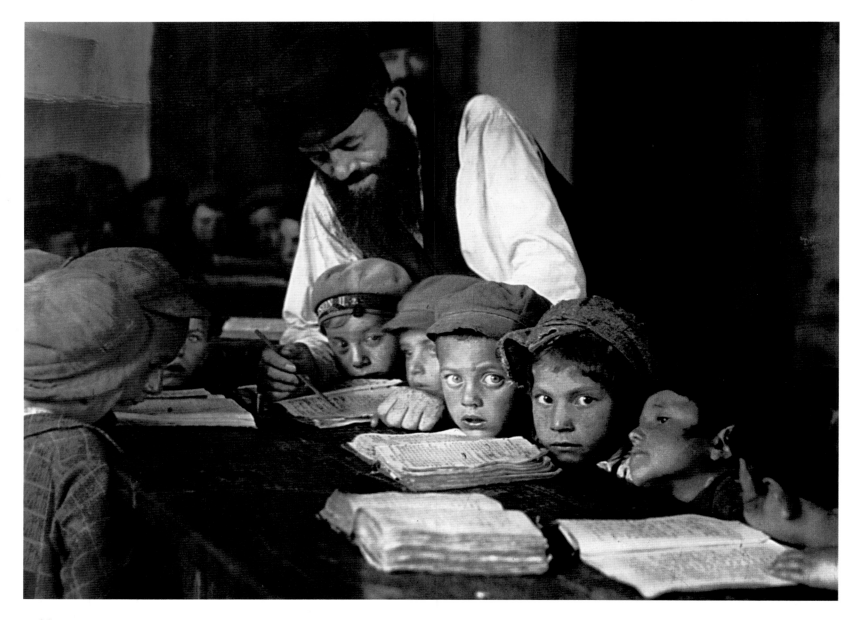

Lublin, 1924

Giving a hint

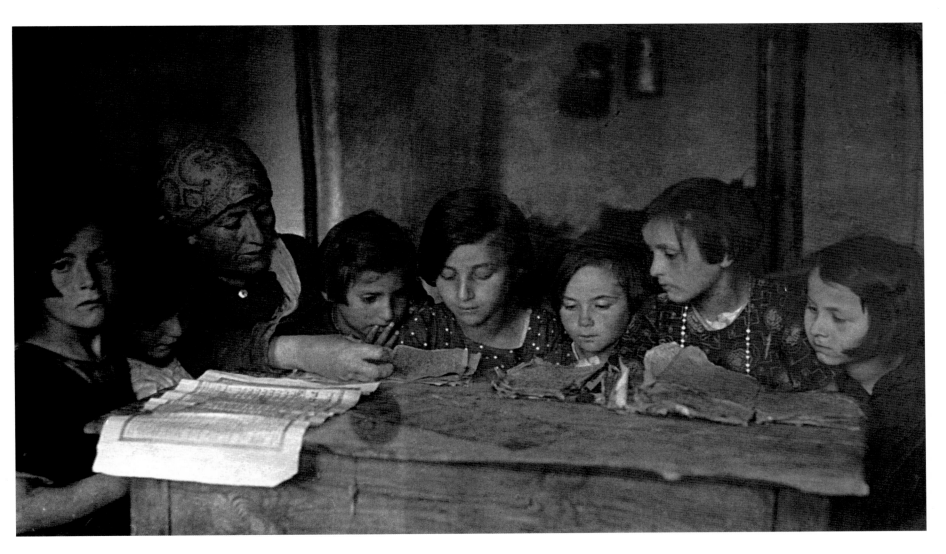

Laskarev (Łaskarzew, Lublin province)

A girls' *kheyder*

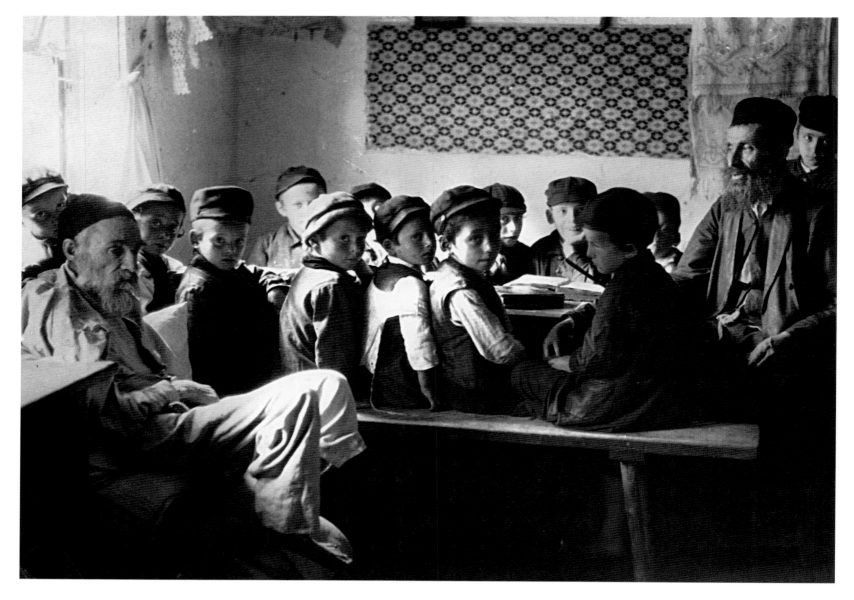

Długosiodło (Białystok province), 1928

Generations come, generations go: Leyzer Segal with his *kheyder* and his ailing father

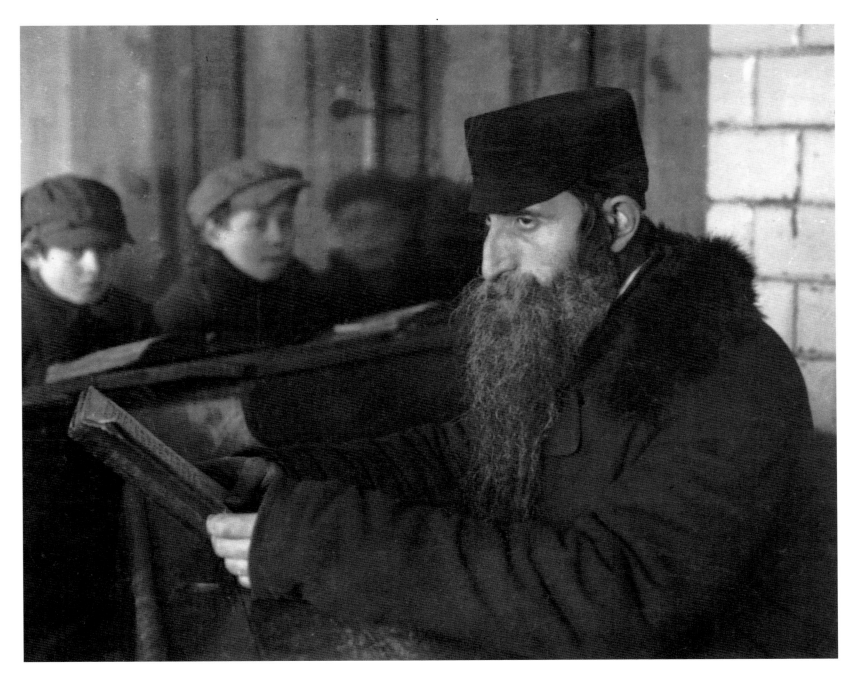

Byale (Biała Podlaska, Lublin province), 1926

The Byaler *melamed*, Binyomin-Hirsh the Beard. More than once his students have nailed his beard—the longest in Byale—to the table when he has dozed off. Perhaps that's why he has such wonderful, sad eyes.

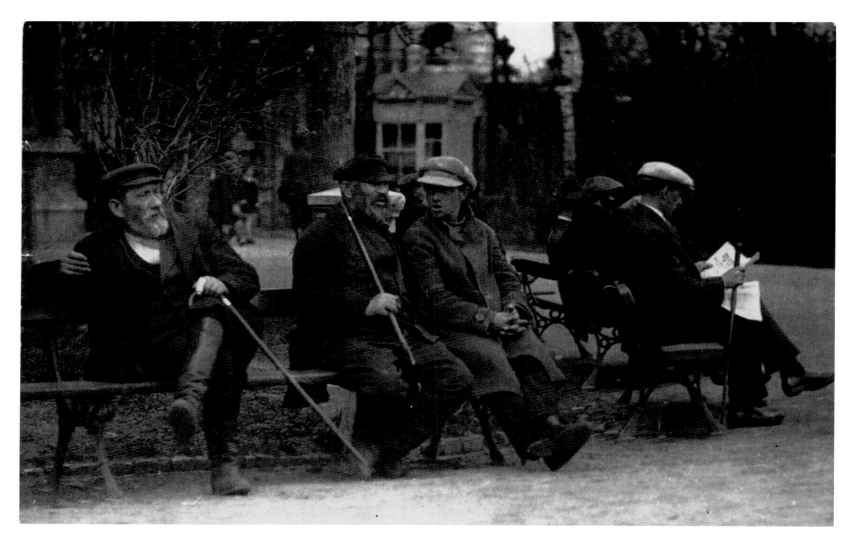

Białystok, 1926
  Jobless weavers taking some air

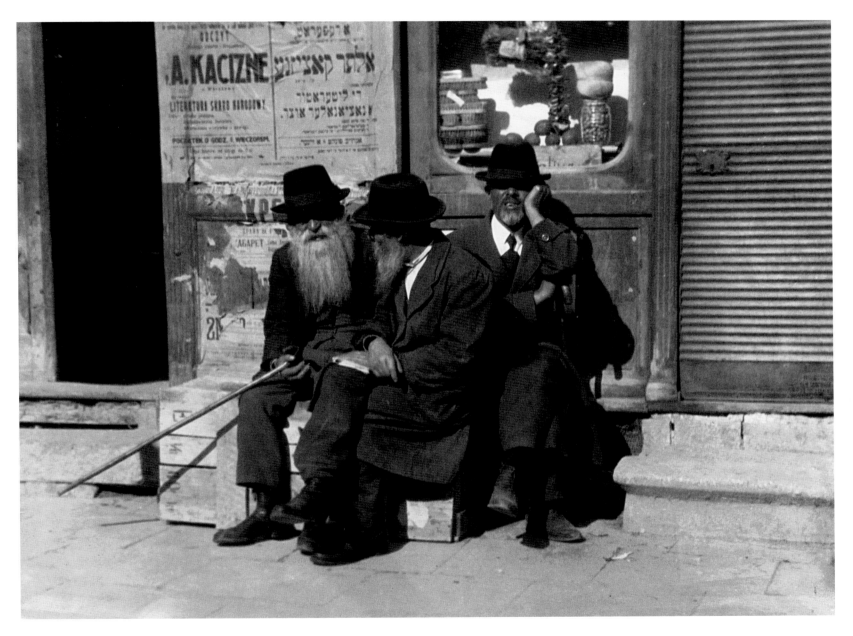

Tshortkev (Czortków, Tarnopol province), 1925

Tshortkever Jews taking a holiday on Sunday, when stores are closed by law.

[On the wall is a poster announcing a lecture by A. Kacyzne on the subject "Literature—A National Treasure."]

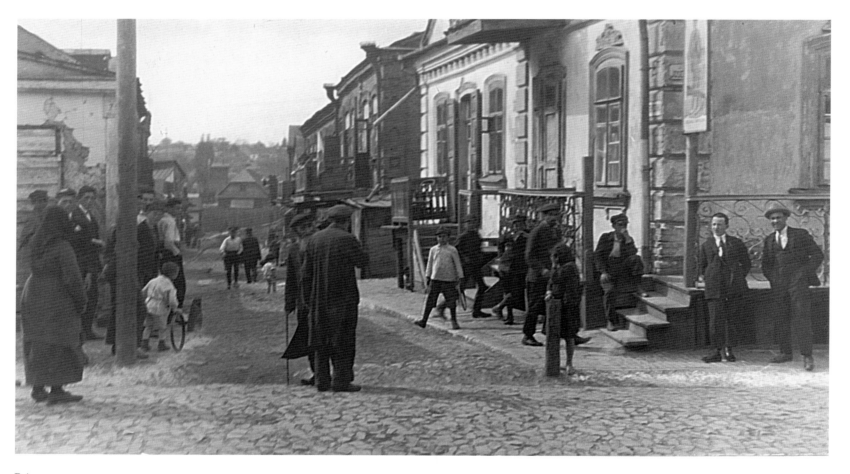

Równe

The Jewish neighborhood on Sunday. The stores are closed.

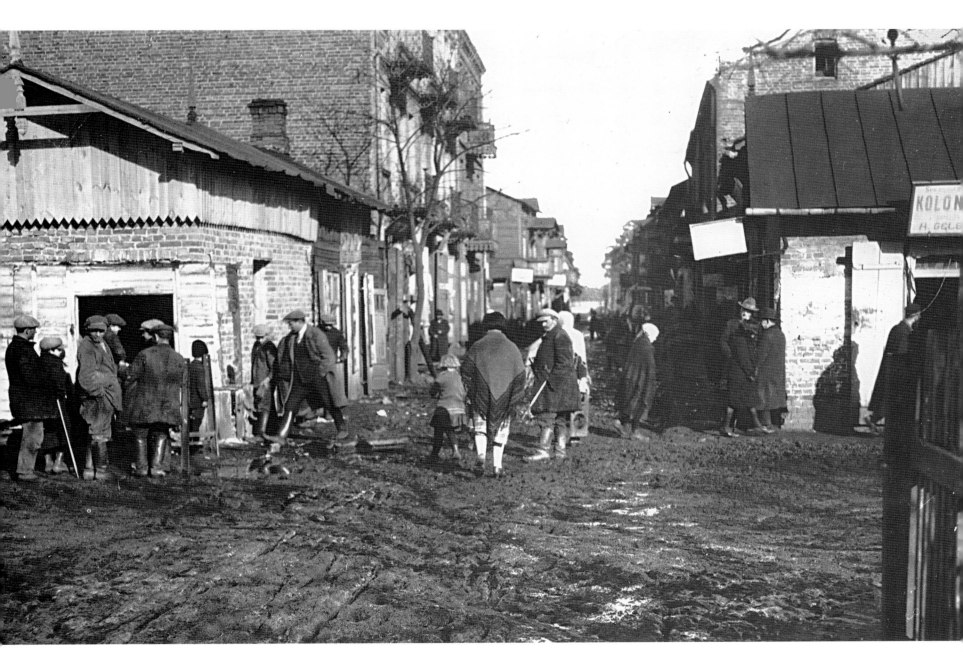

Falenits (Falenica, Warsaw province)

The town's commercial lane

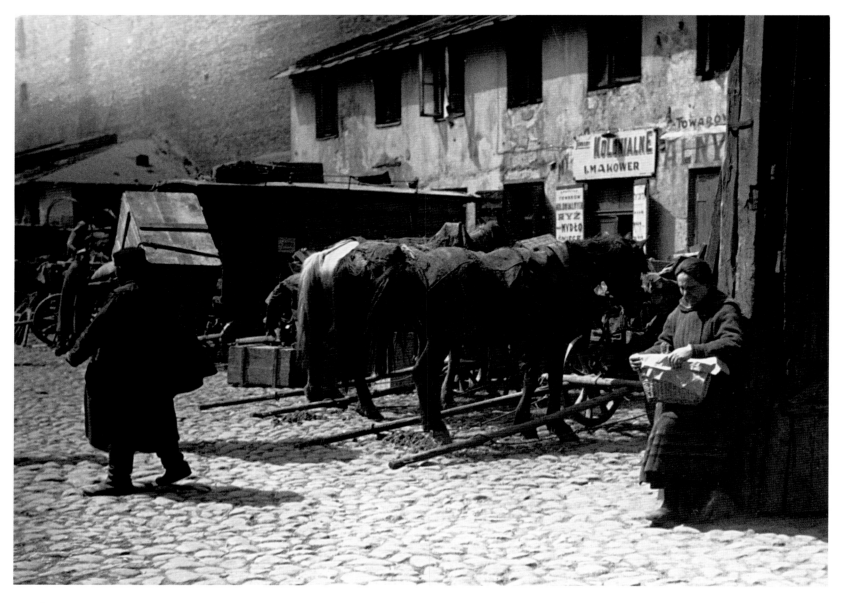

Varshe (Warsaw)

The woman who sells nuts at the entrance to the wagon yard

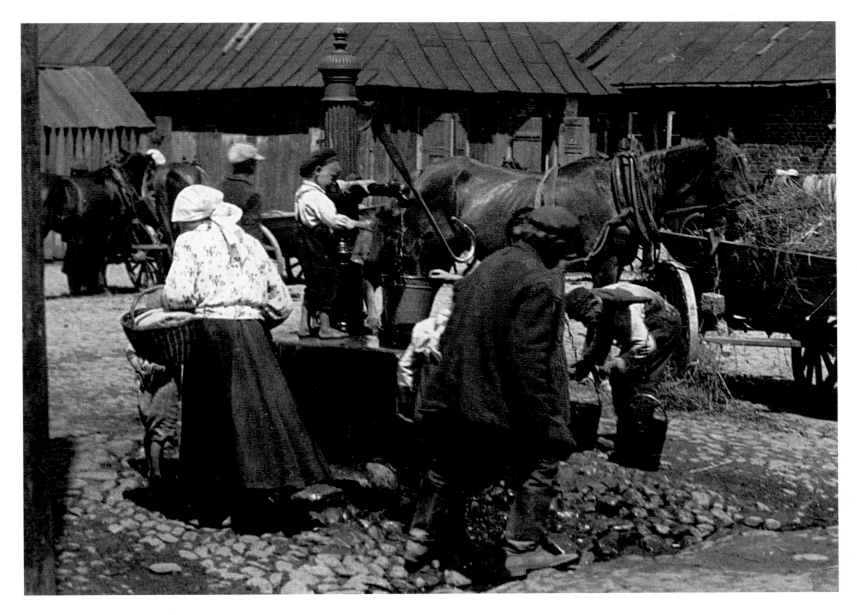

Kozhenits (Kozienice, Kielce province)

At the water pump

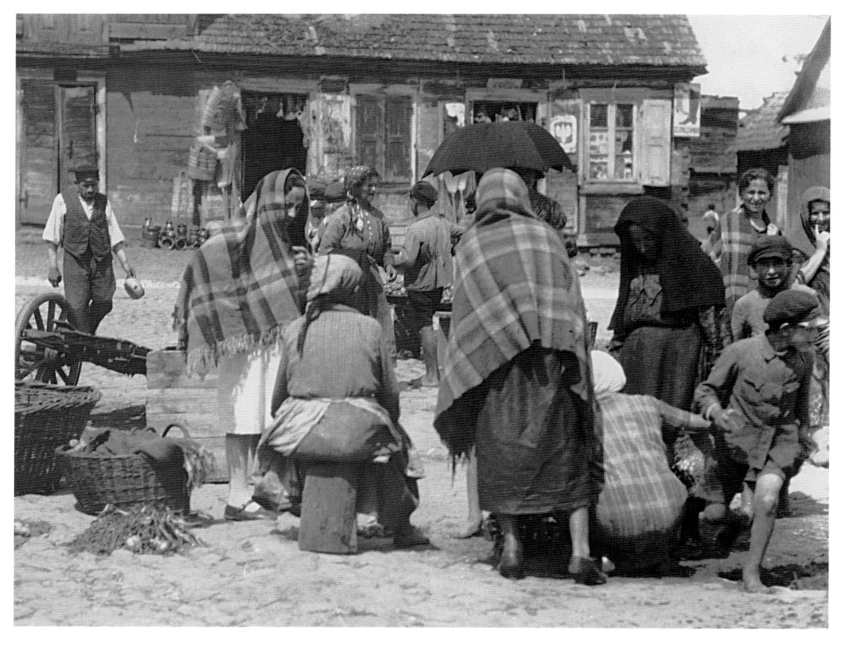

Demblin (Dęblin, Warsaw province)

Monday in Demblin. Make it Friday, if you like.

III

THE
MARKETPLACE

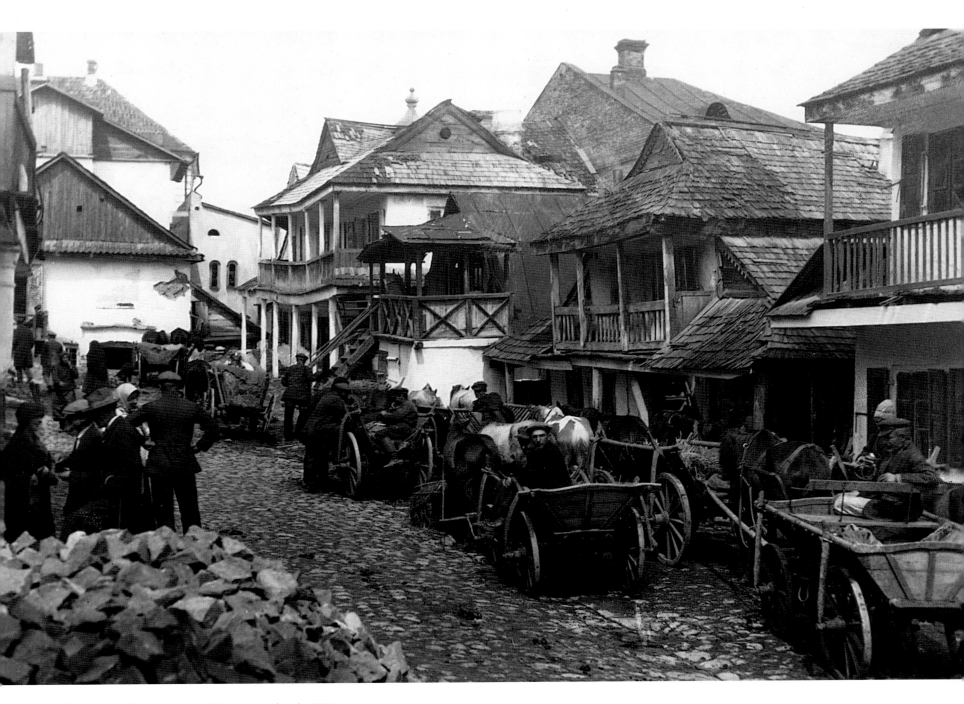

Kremenits (Krzemieniec, Równe province), 1925

The old market

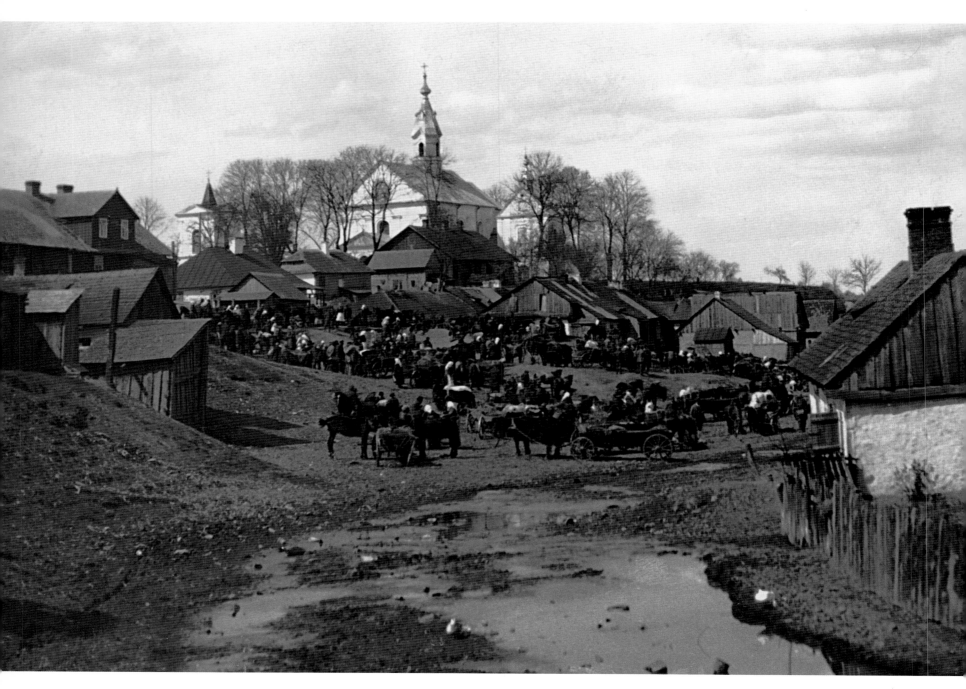

Rubeshoyv (Hrubieszów, Lublin province), 1925

On a market day

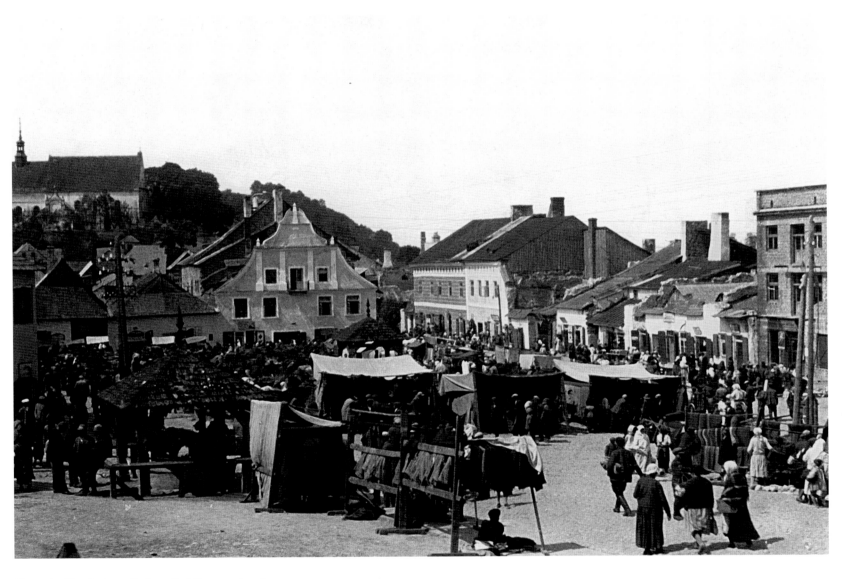

Kuzmir (Kazimierz Dolny, Lublin province)

At the market square

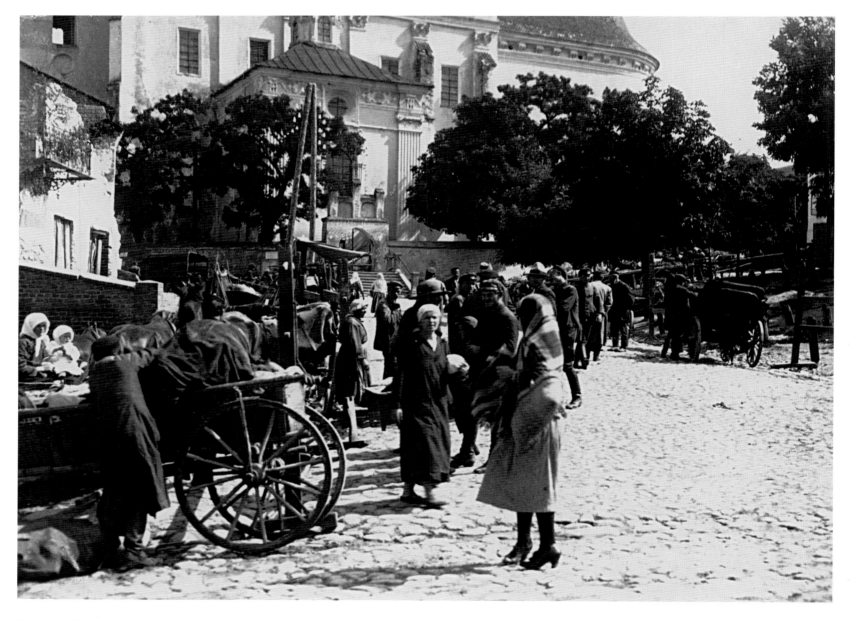

Kuzmir (Kazimierz Dolny, Lublin province)

On a market day, in front of the church

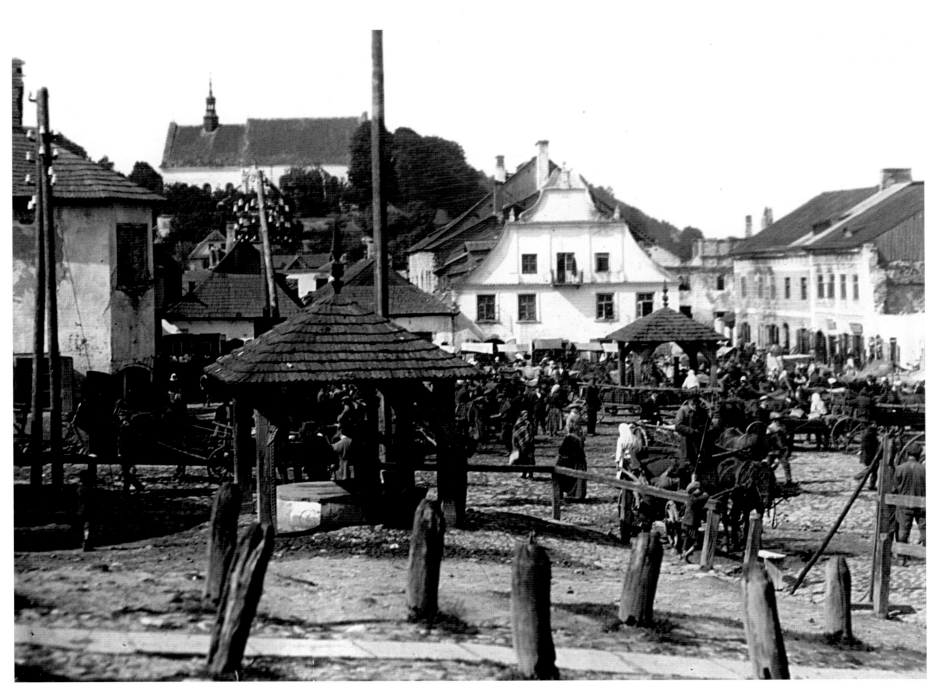

Kuzmir (Kazimierz Dolny, Lublin province)

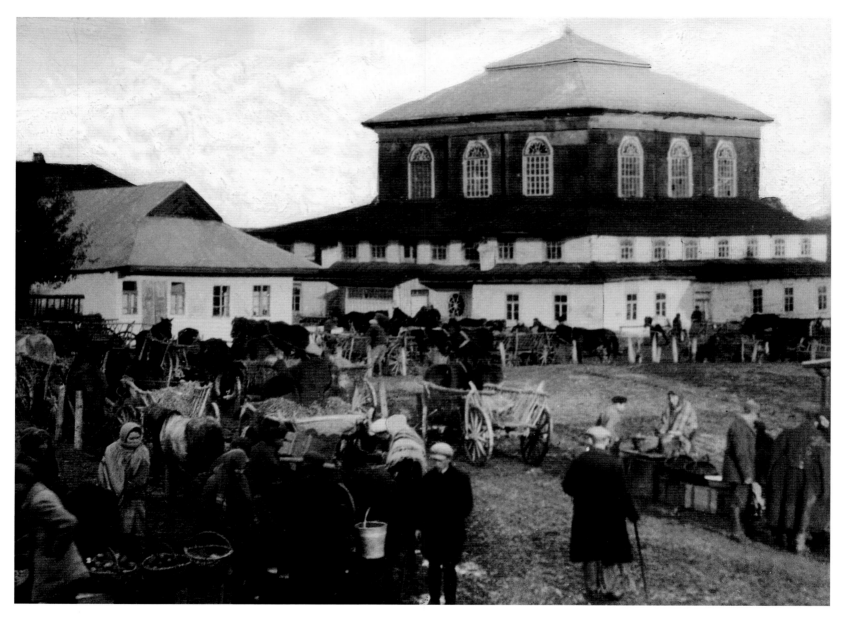

Orkheve (Horochów, Równe province)
  The wooden synagogue in the market square

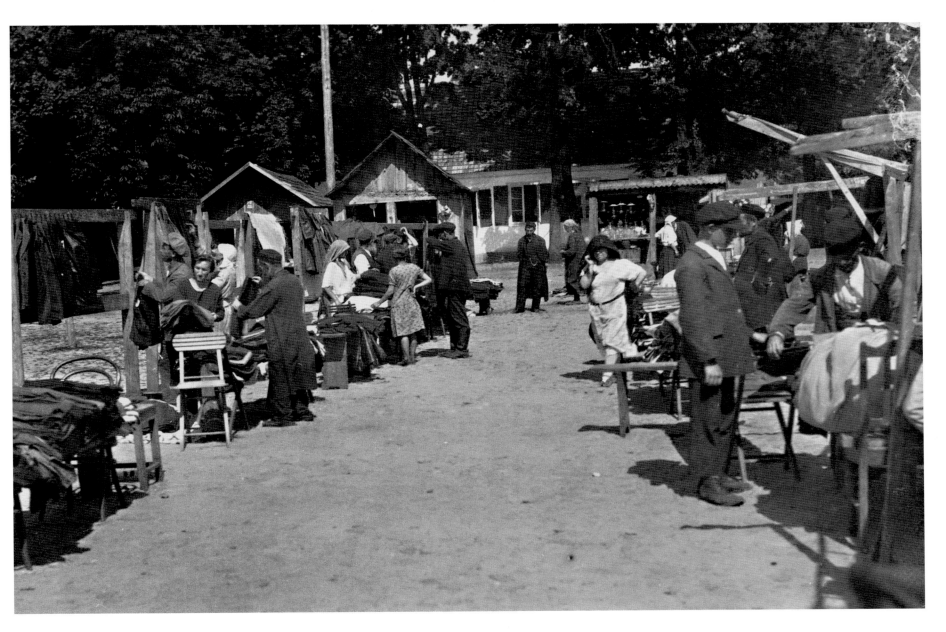

Kozhenits (Kozienice, Kielce province), 1926
  Peddling old clothes

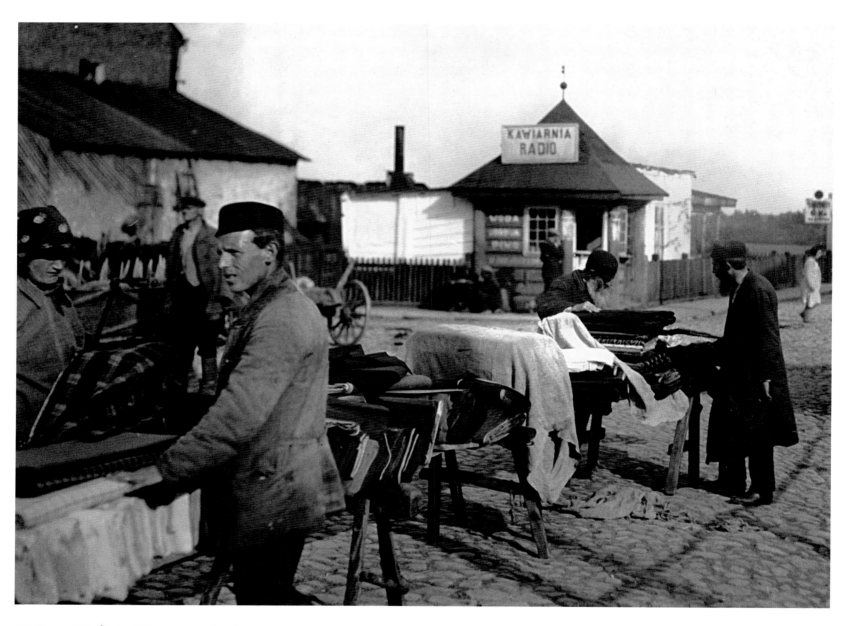

Vishkeve (Wyszków, Warsaw province), 1927

The last customers

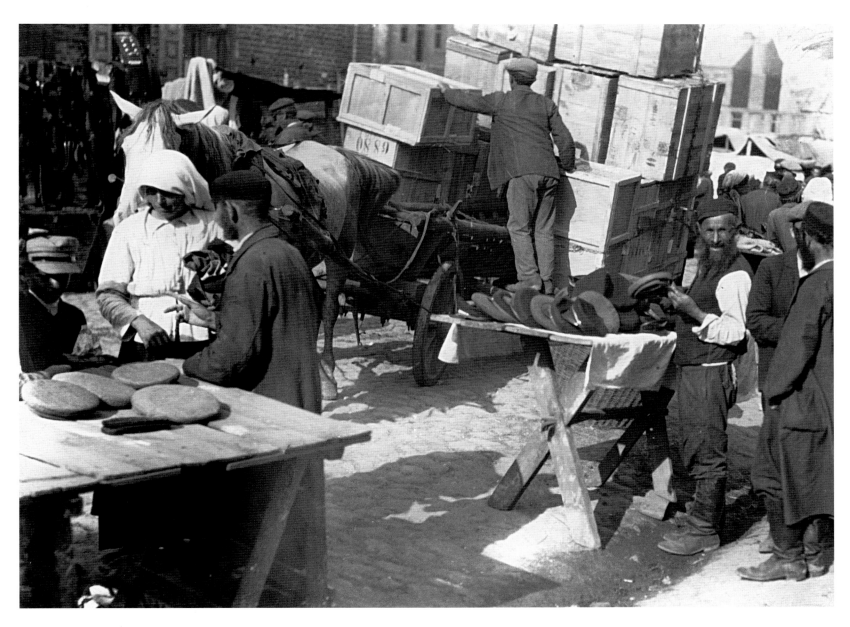

Rike (Ryki, Lublin province)

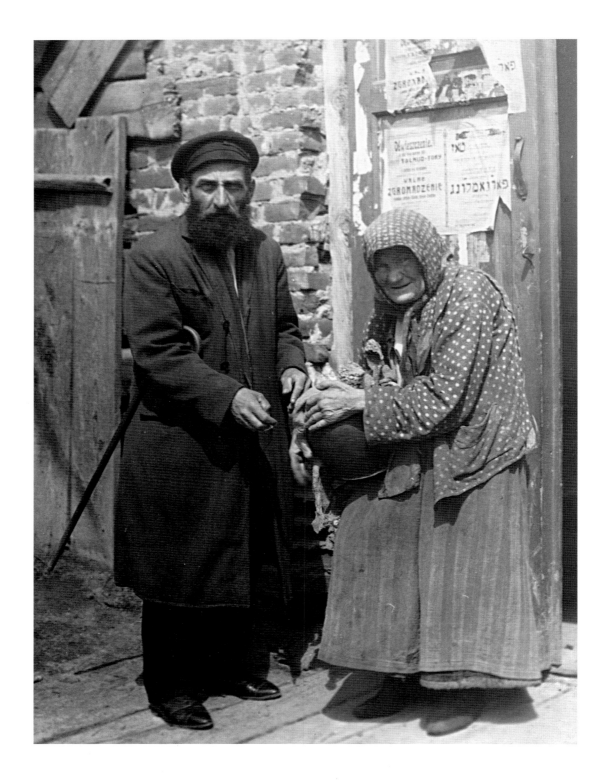

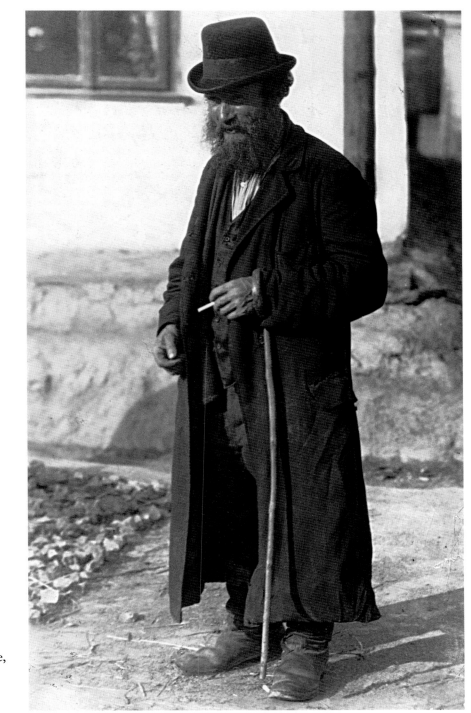

OPPOSITE PAGE

Ostre (Ostróg, Równe province), 1925

There she is, the woman with the hot peas.

Kopitshinits (Kopyczyńce, Tarnopol province)

The cane man. He loiters in the marketplace, looking for odd jobs.

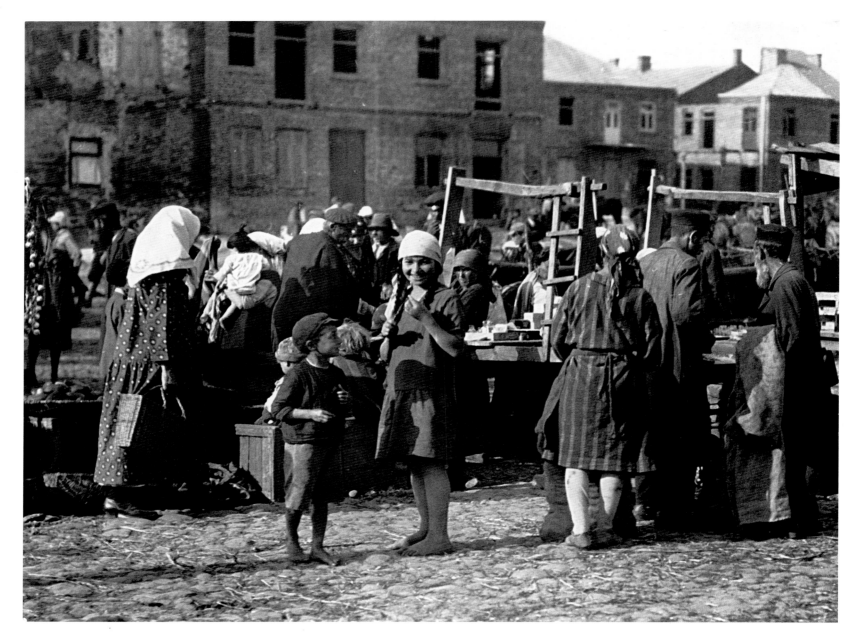

Rike (Ryki, Lublin province)

The little boy wants to know why his sister is smiling (she has noticed the camera and he has not).

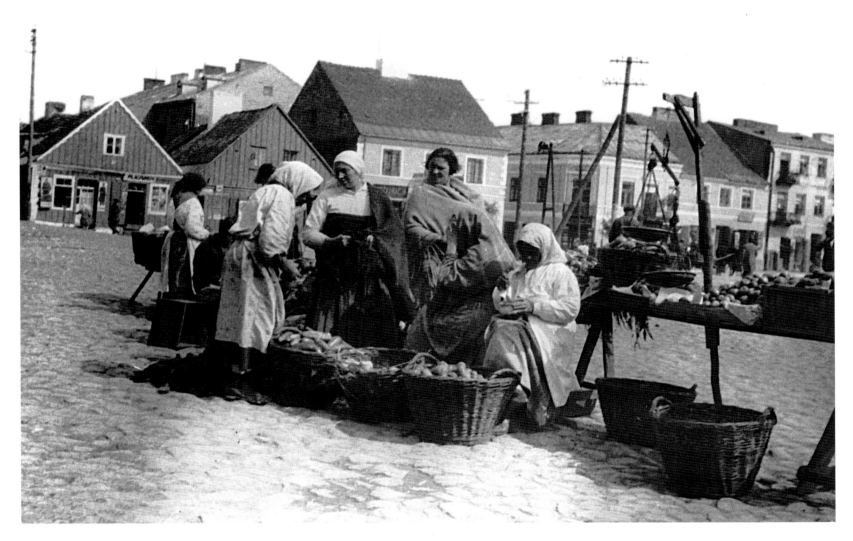

Hlinsk (Glińsko, Lwów province)

    Balebostes

        [Housewives]

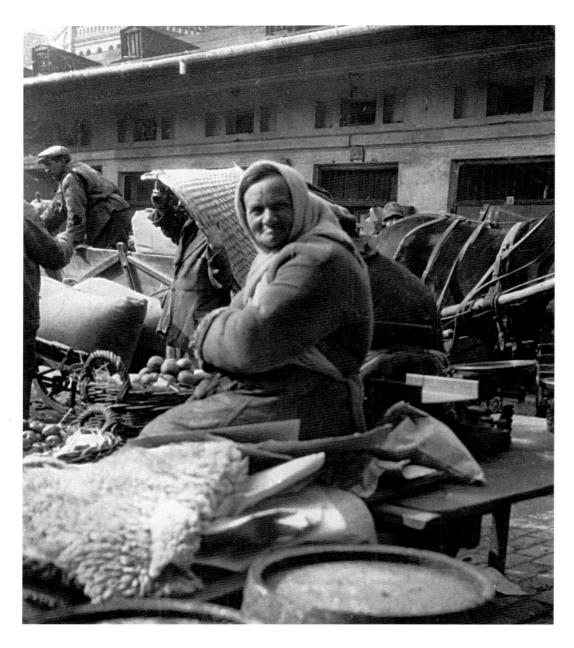

y

w

Varshe (Warsaw)

Near the Warsaw *Hales*

[The Hala Mirowska was an indoor market.]

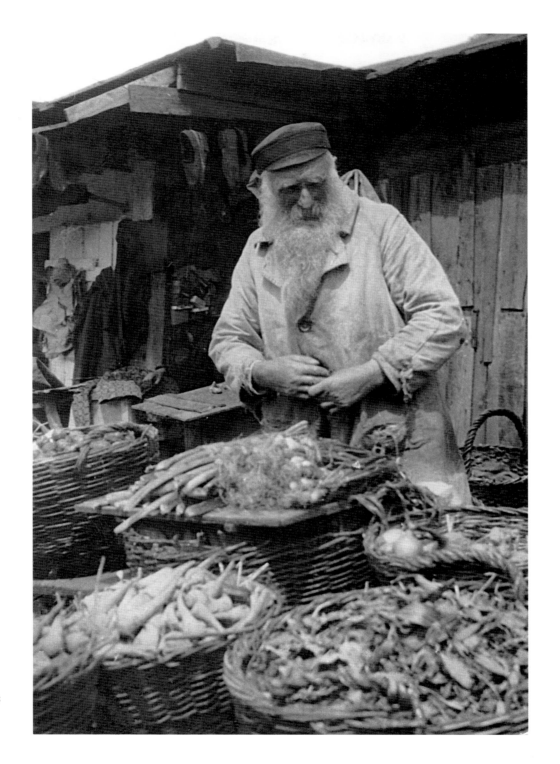

Selling herbs

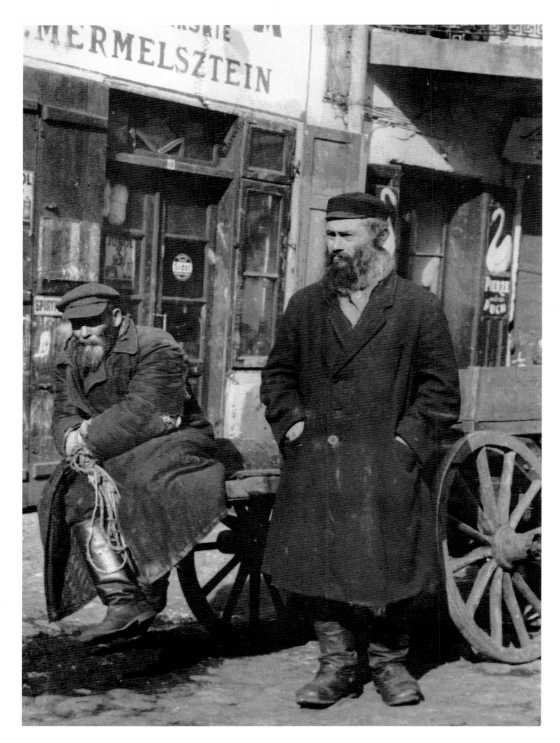

Varshe (Warsaw)

Street people: one way or the other, something will turn up.

OPPOSITE PAGE

The bookkeeping

OVERLEAF

Kolomey (Kołomyja, Stanisławów province)

The marketplace

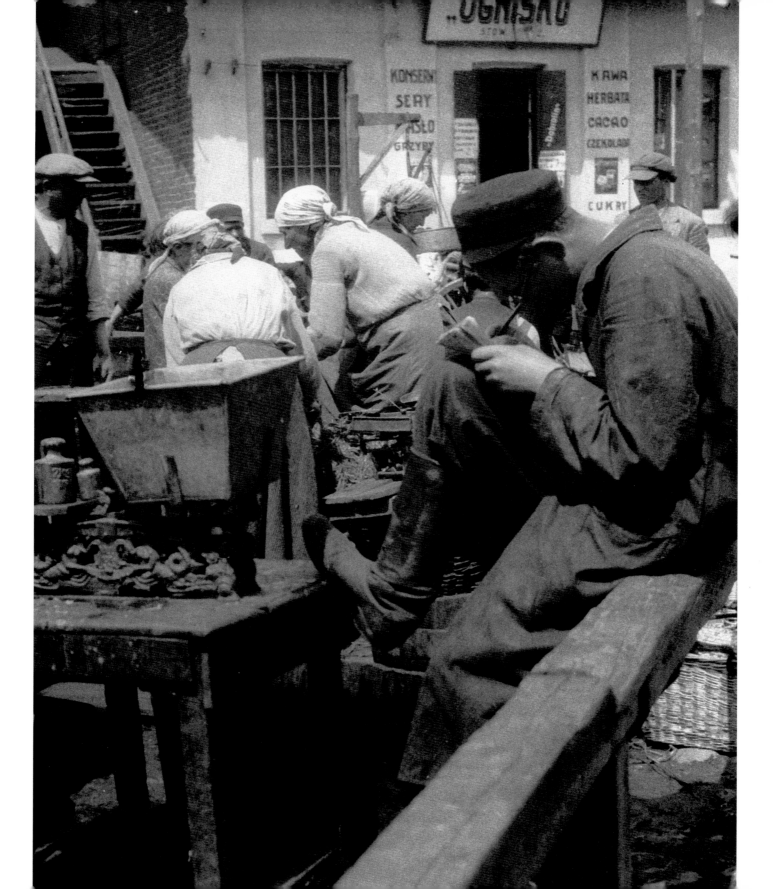

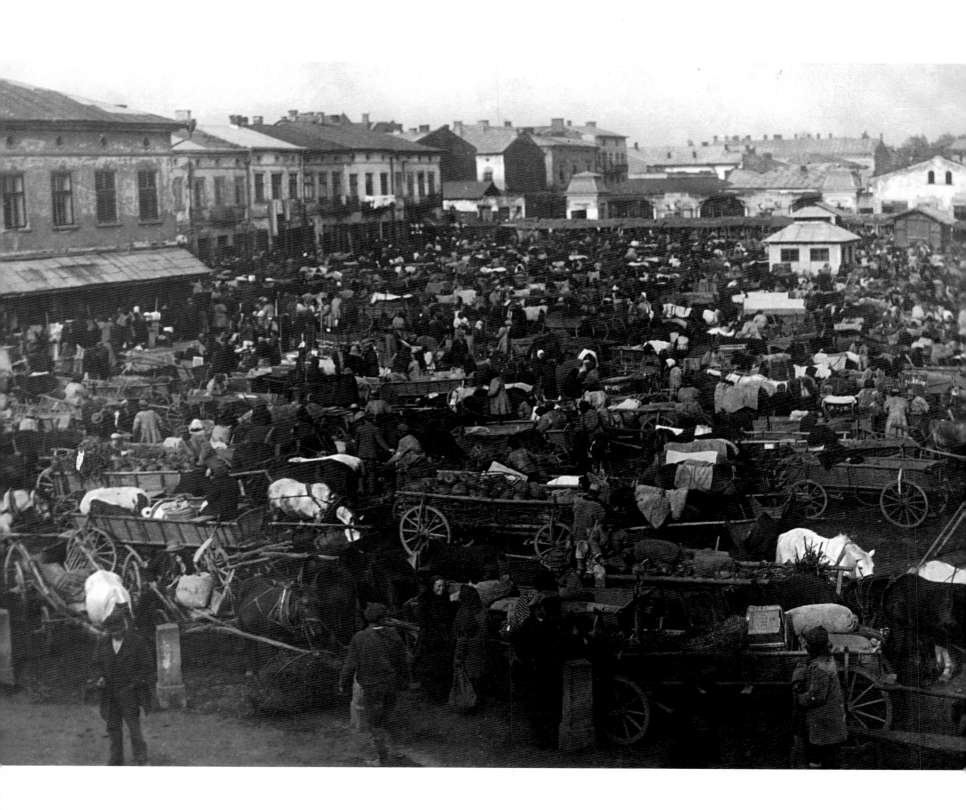

IV

AT WORK

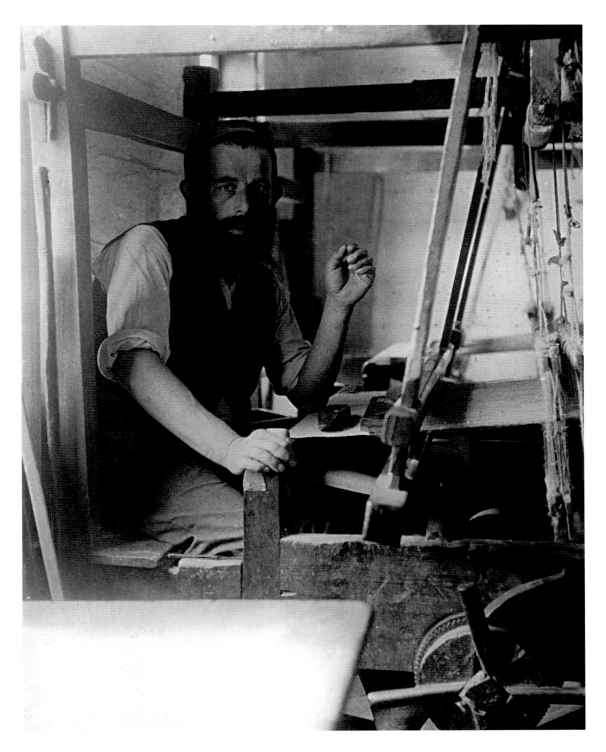

Vonvolnits (Wąwolnica, Lublin province), 1925

Yisroel Lustman, a linen weaver

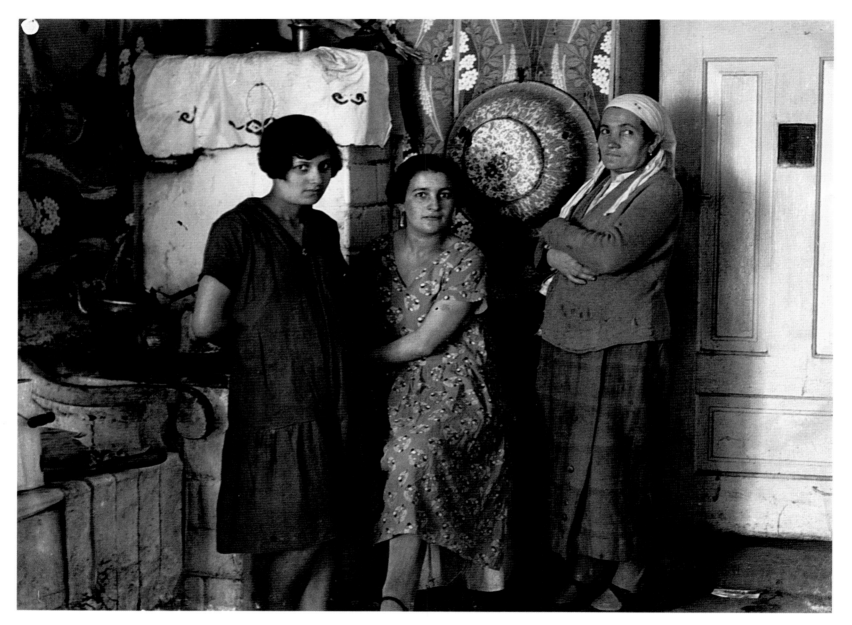

Wołomin (Warsaw province), 1927

Malke-Reyzl with her daughters. They sell bread.

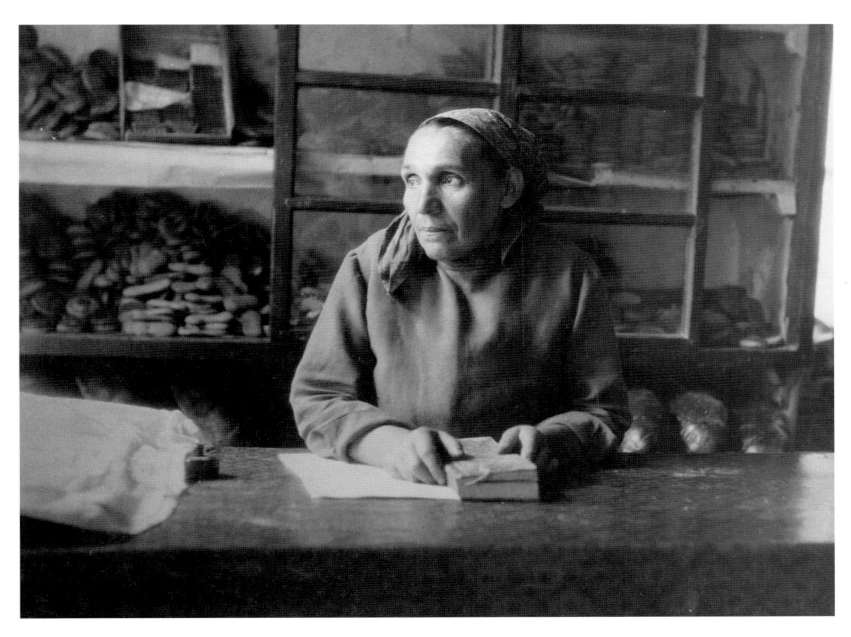

Wilejka (Wilno province)
  Sara, the baker's wife

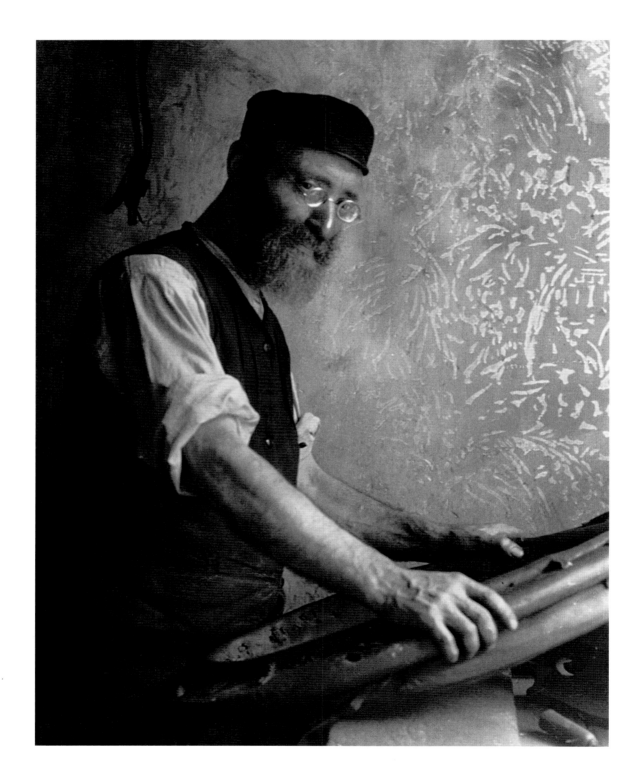

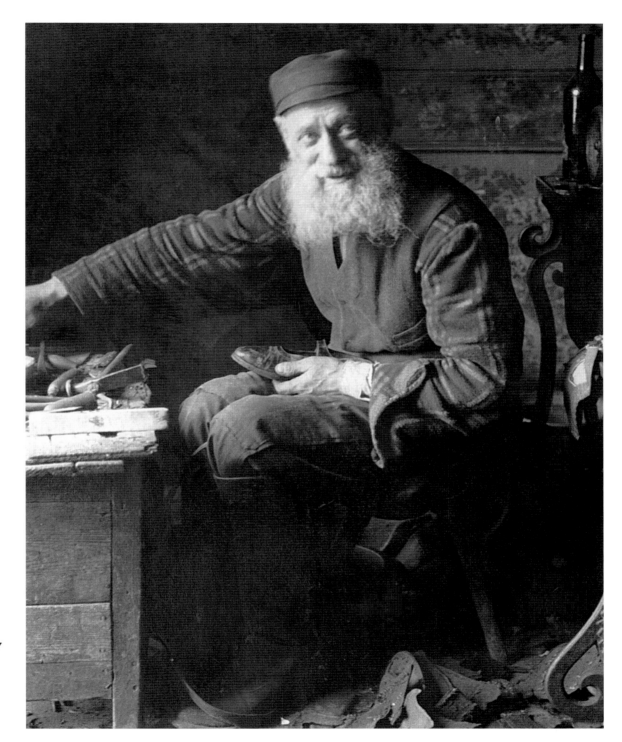

OPPOSITE PAGE
Wołomin (Warsaw province)
Jakub Ścierański, a saddler

Varshe (Warsaw), 1927
The optimist
[A cobbler]

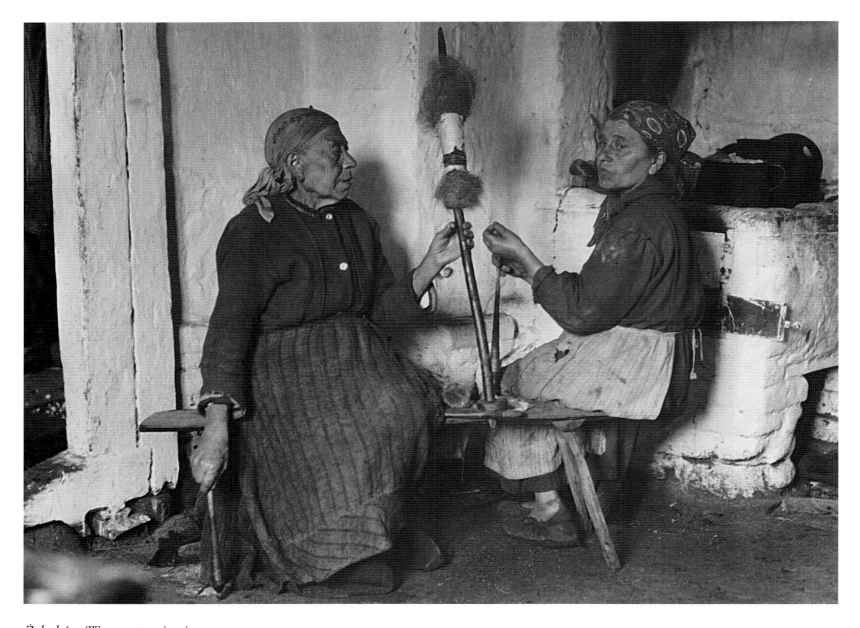

Żelechów (Warsaw province)

Feyge, Motl the *melamed*'s niece, eighty-five years old. She spins flax with her daughter.

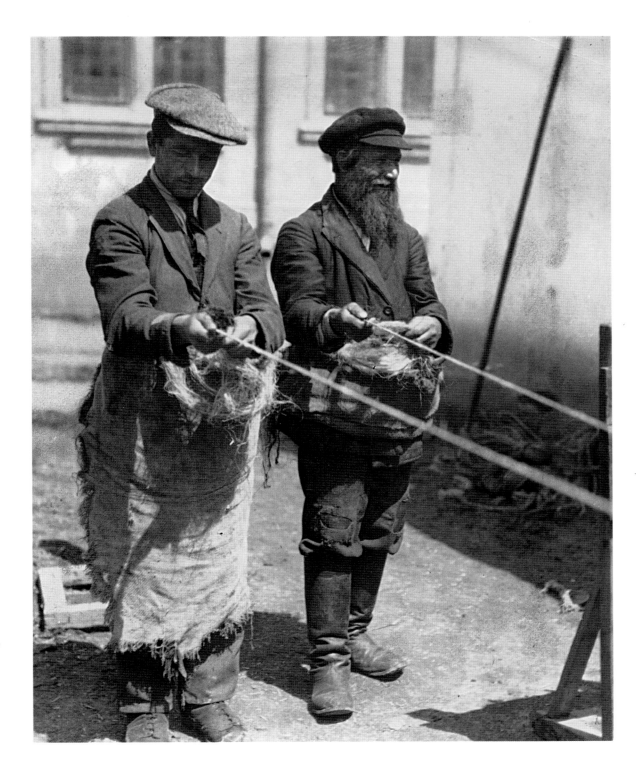

Kopitshinits (Kopyczyńce, Tarnopol province), 1925

A Jewish trade. Rope spinners, father and son.

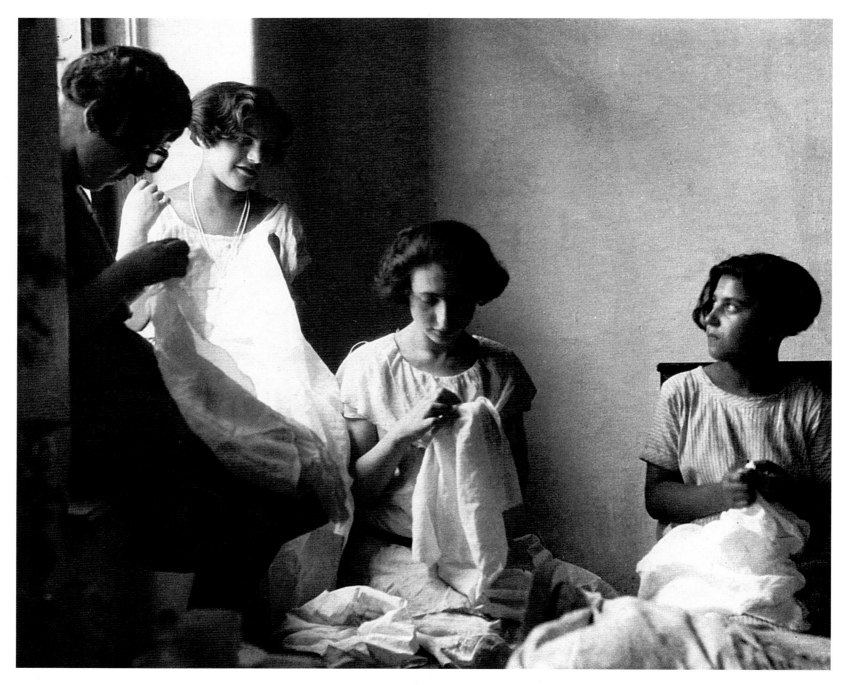

Kozhenits (Kozienice, Kielce province), 1927

Embroidery is a popular trade in this town.

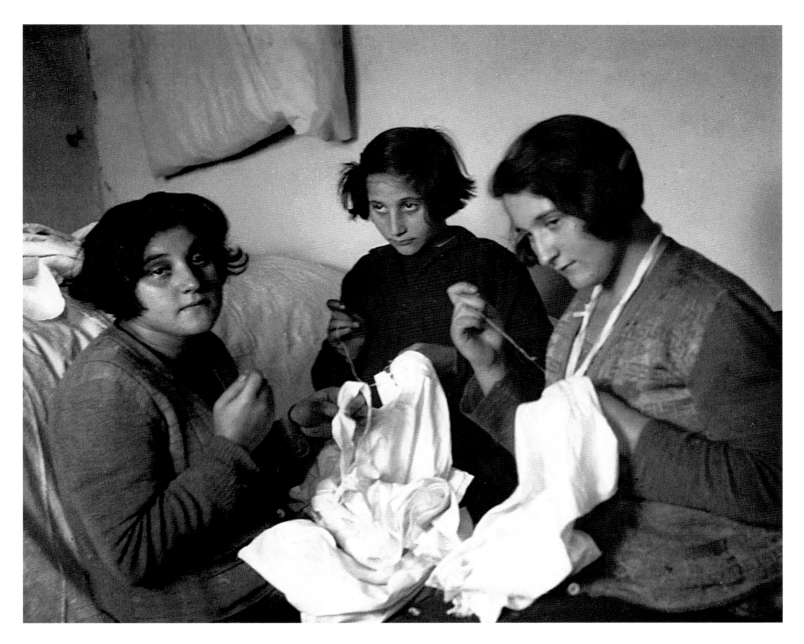

Nowy Dwór (Warsaw province), 1927

"Three girls are sitting and sewing."   —I. L. Peretz

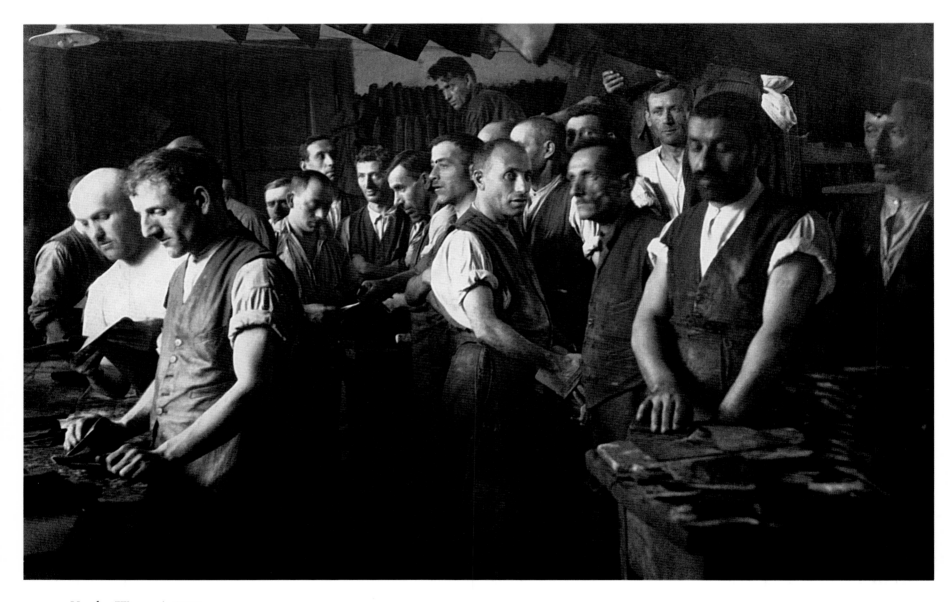

Varshe (Warsaw), 1929

A Bundist leather workers' cooperative

[The Bund was the largest Jewish Socialist party in Poland.]

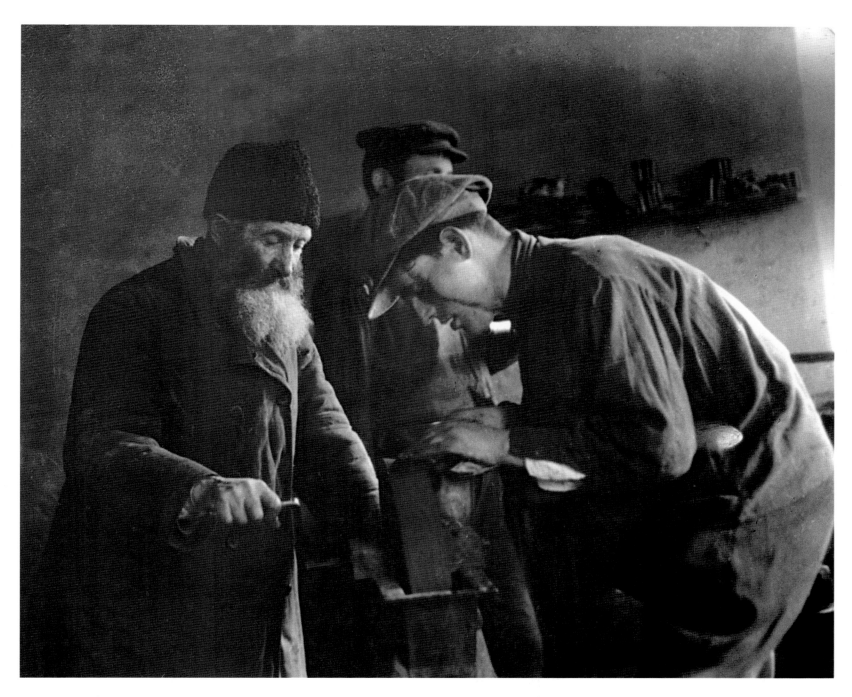

Visoke Litovsk (Wysokie Litewskie, Pińsk province), 1927
  At work in the mechanical shop

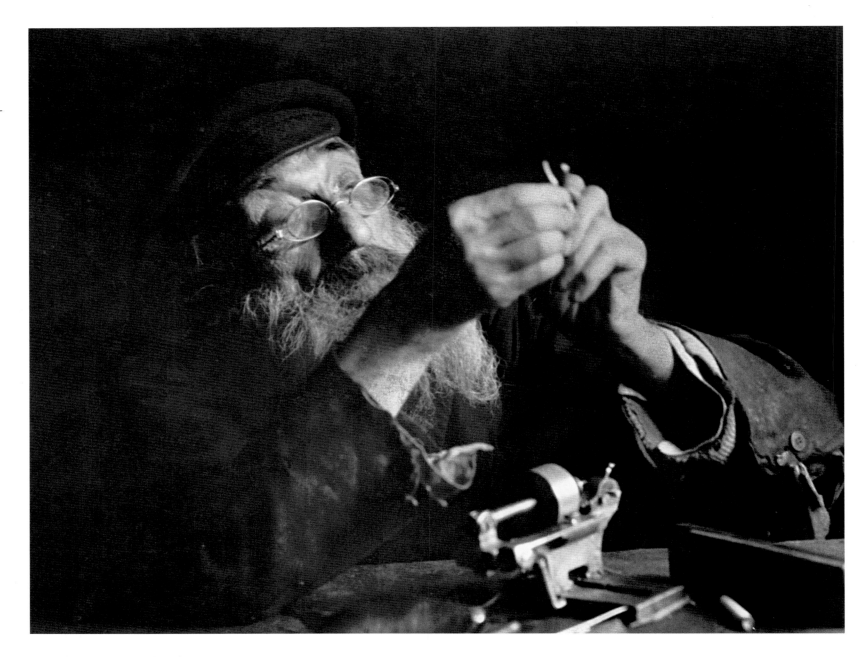

Lomzhe (Łomża, Białystok province), 1927

   Khone Shlayfer, eighty-five years old. Besides being a *shlayfer*, a grinder, he is also a
mechanic, an umbrella maker, and a medicine man (he really does deserve a full page).

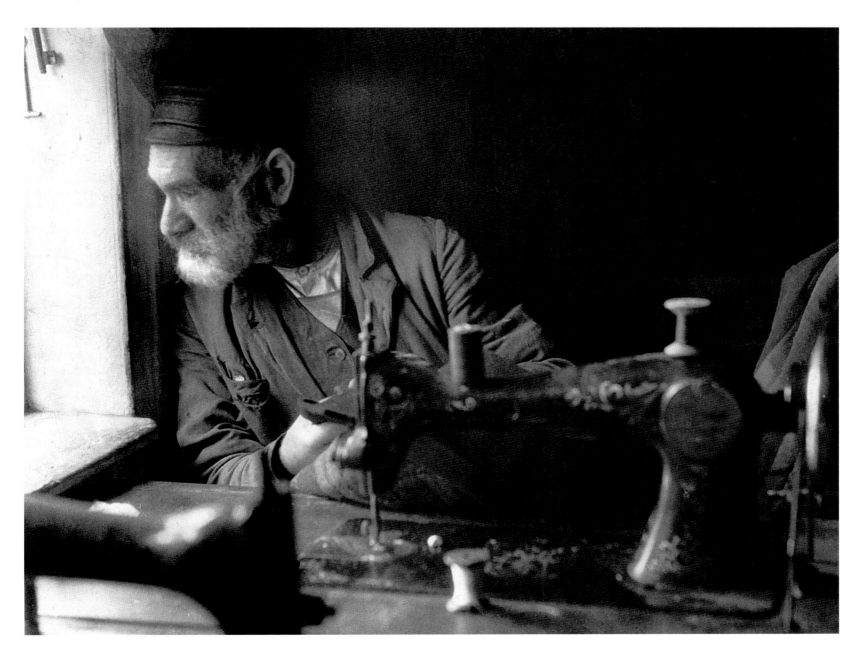

Kutne (Kutno, Warsaw province), 1927
   Aron-Nokhem at his sewing machine

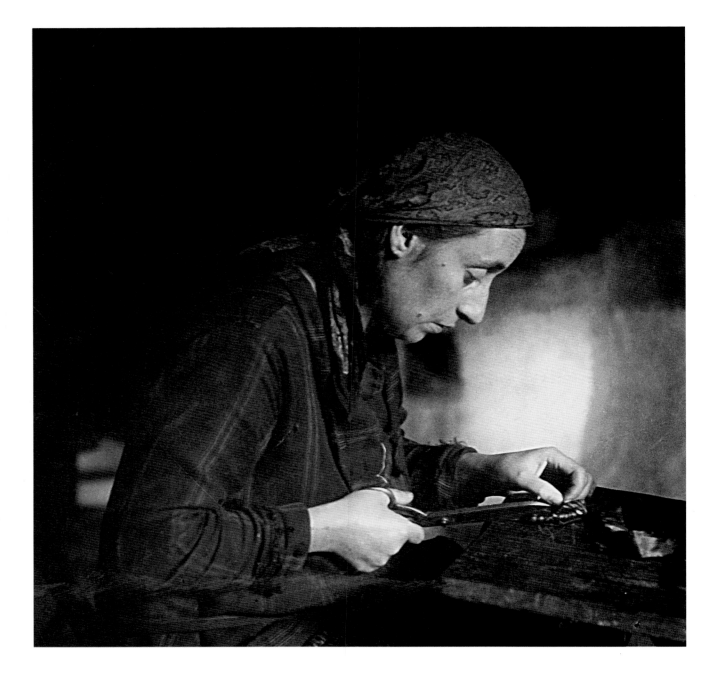

Purisov (Parysów, Lublin province), 1927

Esther at work. Her husband left her seven years ago with five children,
whom she supports working as a seamstress.

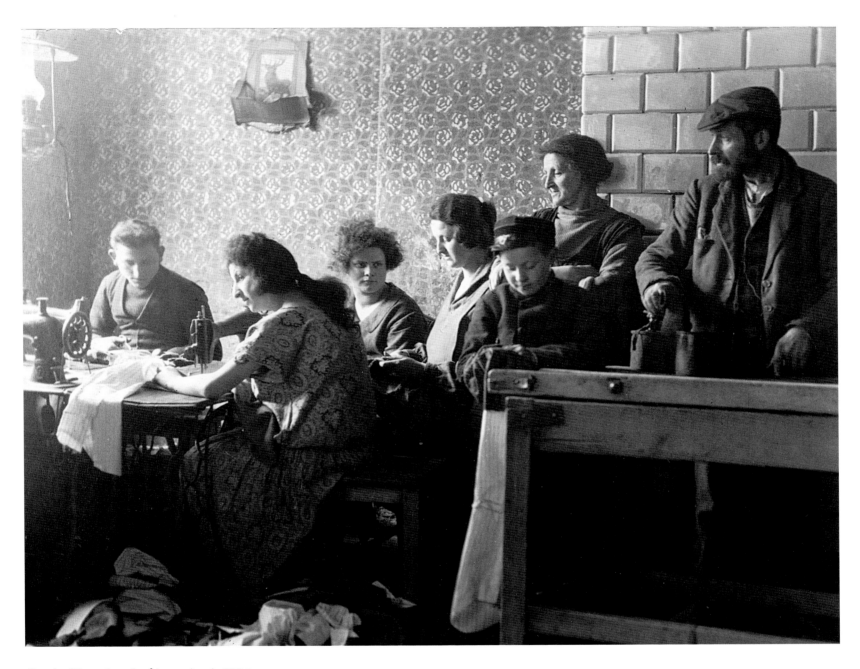

Brezin (Brzeziny, Łodź province), 1926

A happy tailor. He works with his family.

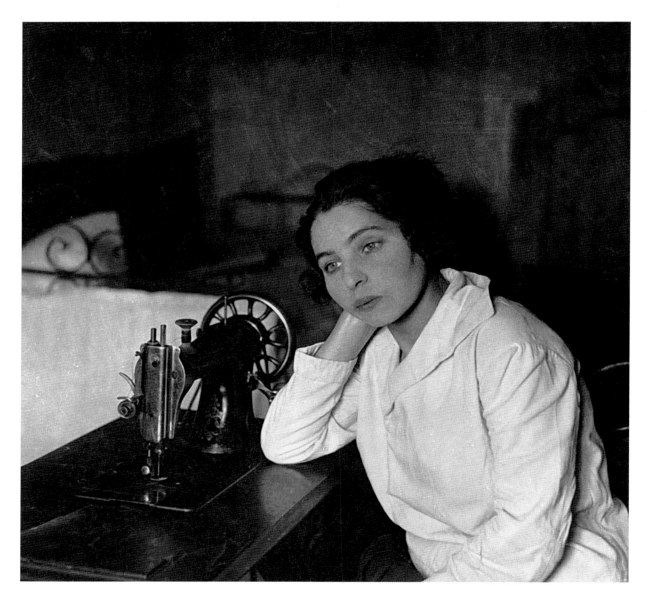

Białystok, 1926

The unemployed seamstress

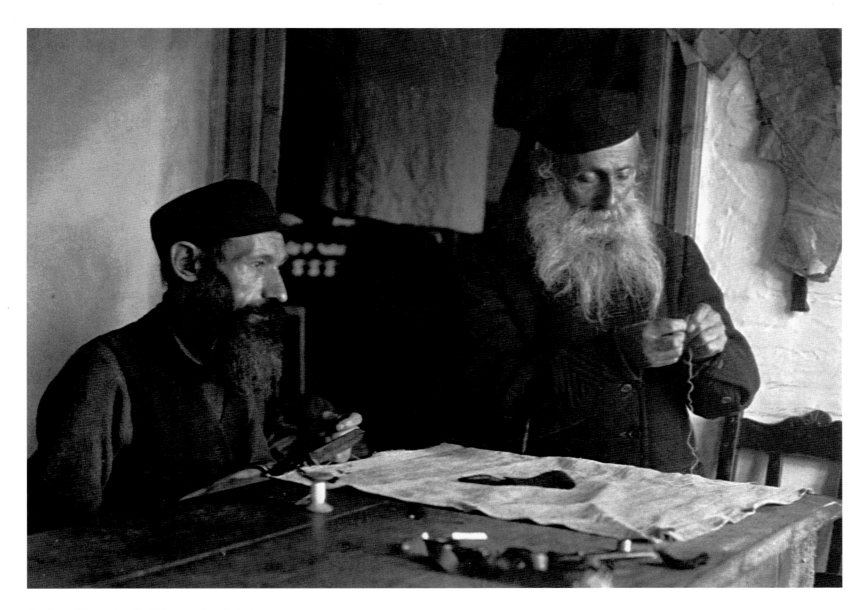

Purisov (Parysów, Lublin province), 1926

At ninety-three, this village tailor can thread the needle without wearing glasses.

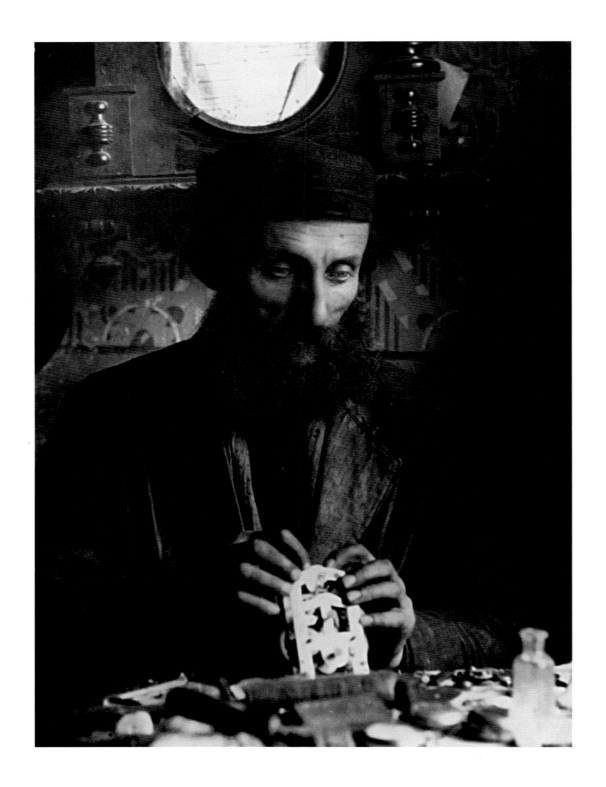

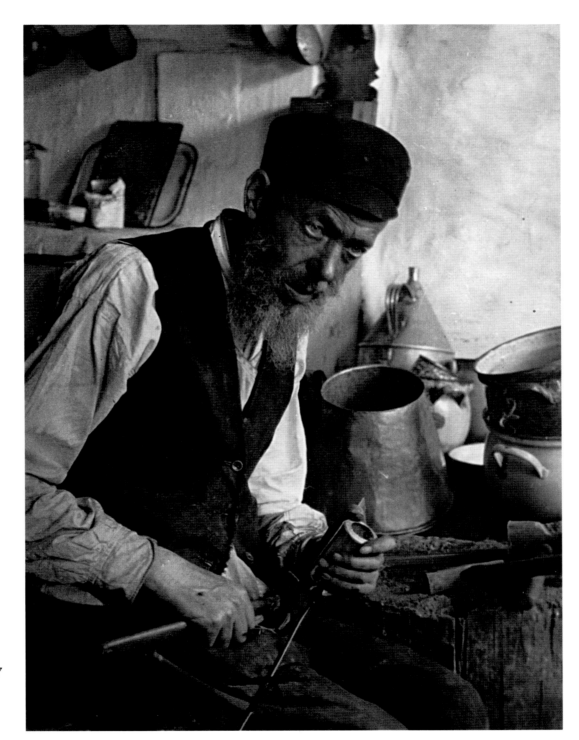

Ger (Góra Kalwaria, Warsaw province)
Naftule Grinband and his clocks

Garwolin (Lublin province), 1927
A tinsmith

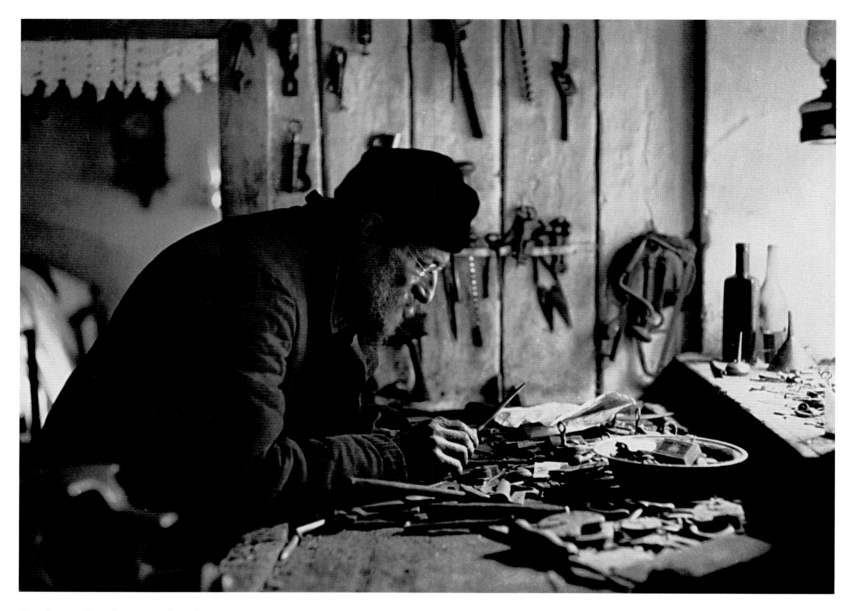

Zambrove (Zambrów, Białystok province)

The locksmith Eliyohu. He has been blind in one eye for twelve years but agreed to have surgery only after he went blind in the other eye too.

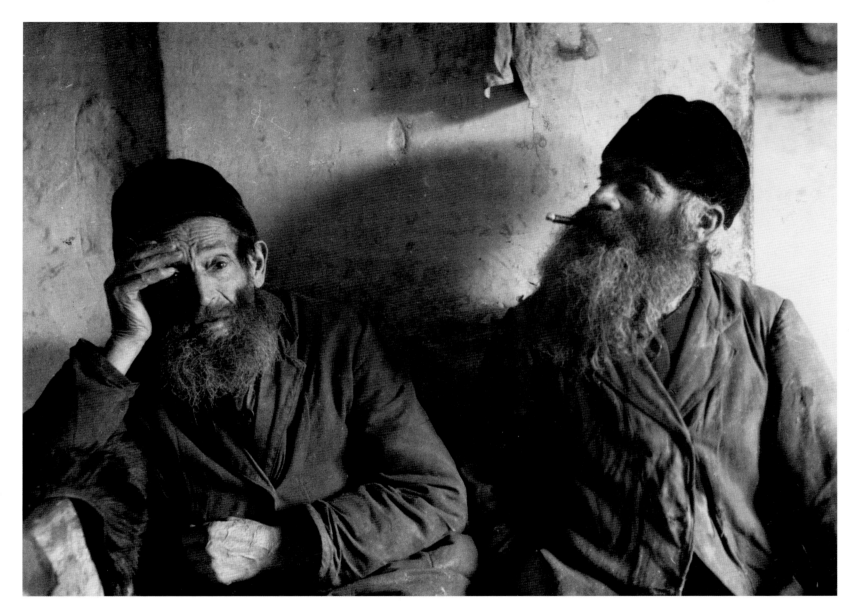

Byale (Biała Podlaska, Lublin province), 1926

Father and son. To protect himself from the Evil One, Leyzer Bawół, the blacksmith, will not say how old he is, but he must be over one hundred. Now his son does the smithing and the old man has become a doctor. He sets broken arms and legs.

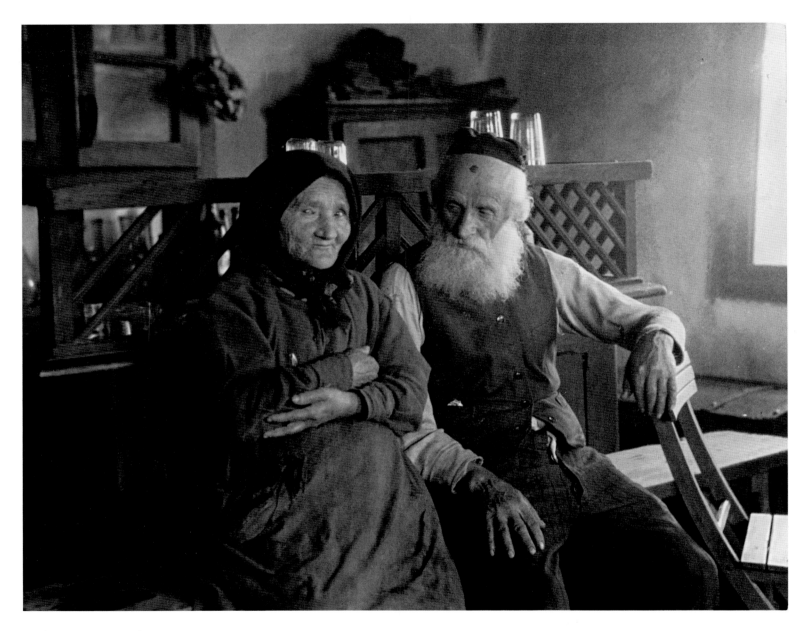

Suchostaw (Tarnopol province)
  The tavern keeper and his wife

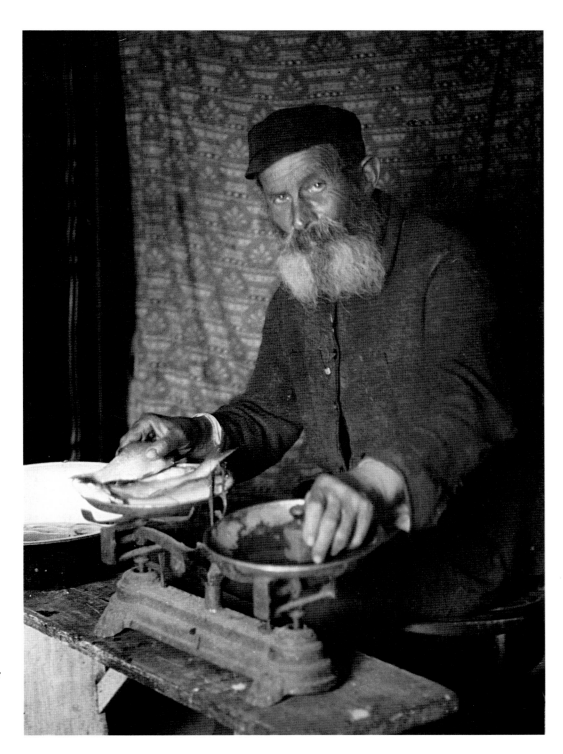

Jabłonka (Białystok province), 1927
Meyer Kon, the fishmonger

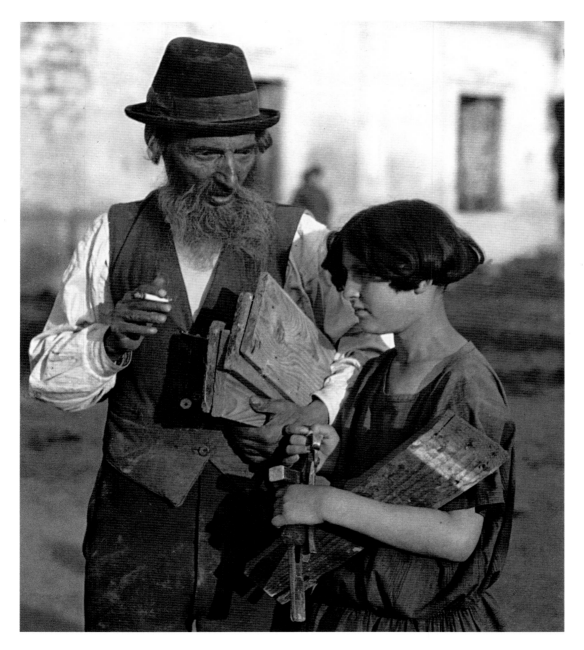

OPPOSITE PAGE

Varshe (Warsaw)

They grab their merchandise by the ears and flee at the sight of a policeman.

Tshortkev (Czortków, Tarnopol province), 1925

The carpenter and his granddaugher

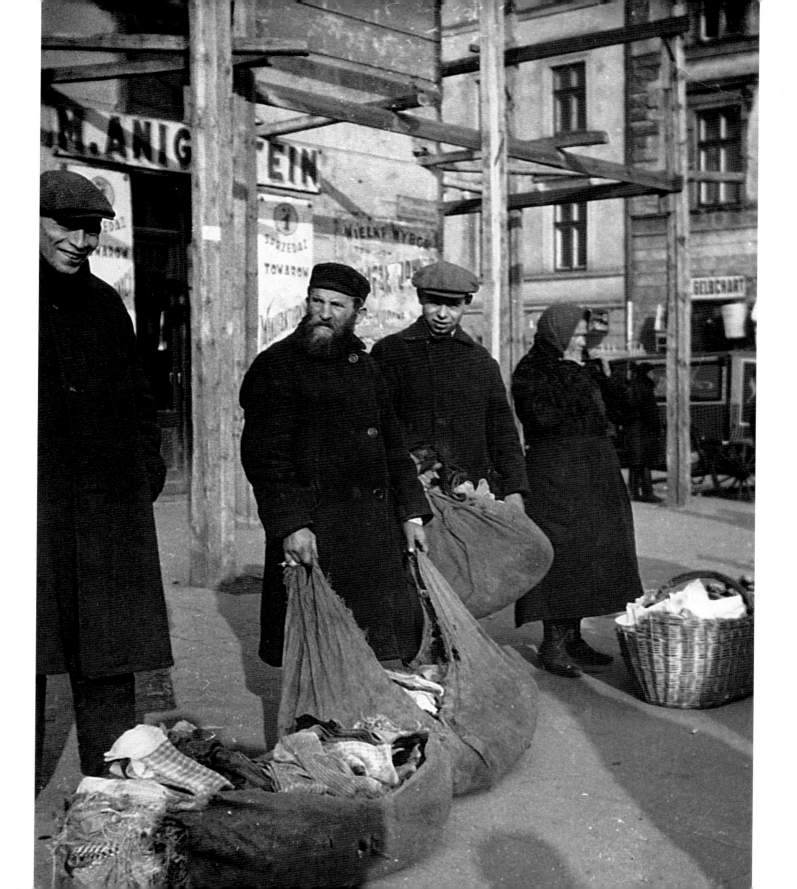

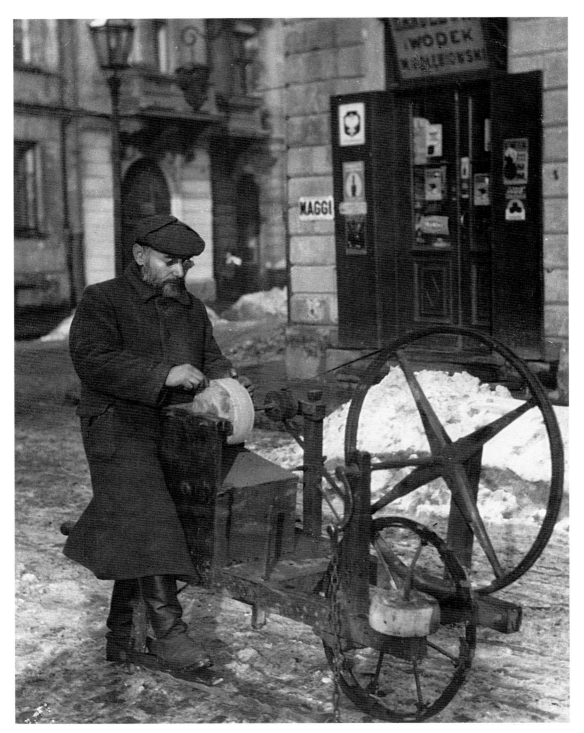

Varshe (Warsaw), 1928

What did he fight for? Fayvl Tabakman, a former political prisoner, can find no work as a locksmith. So he walks the streets and sharpens knives.

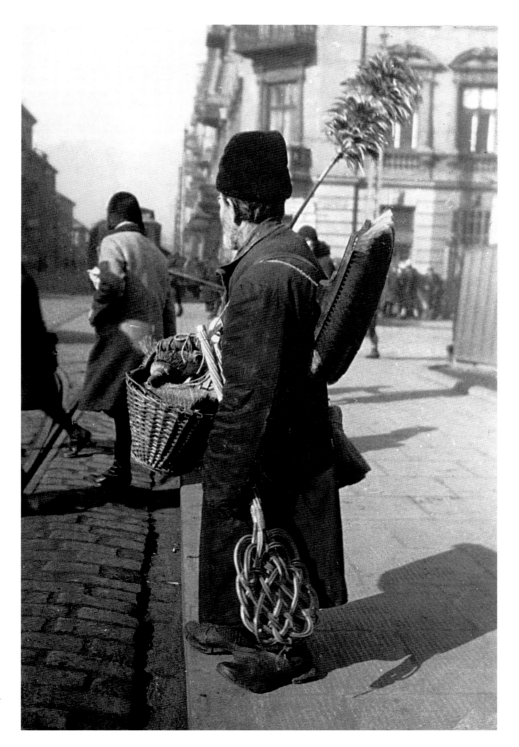

Rugbeater in full regalia

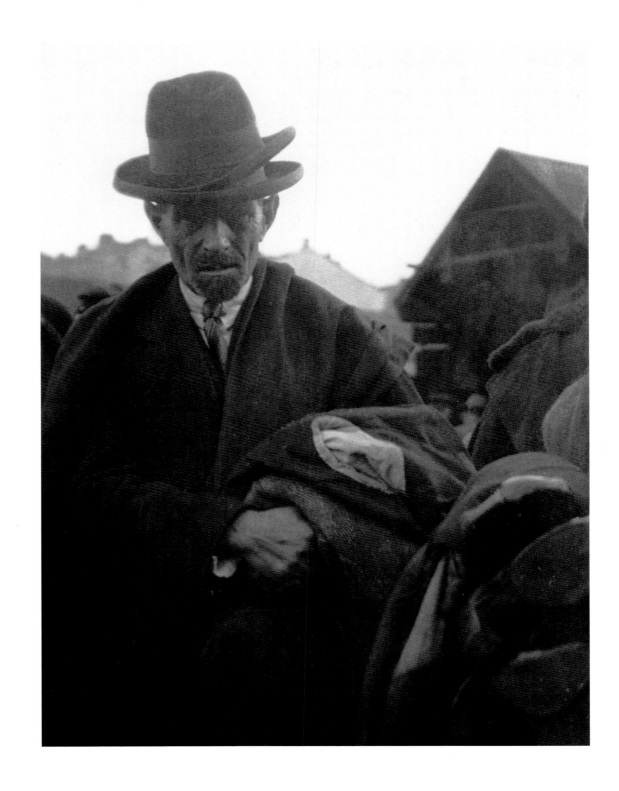

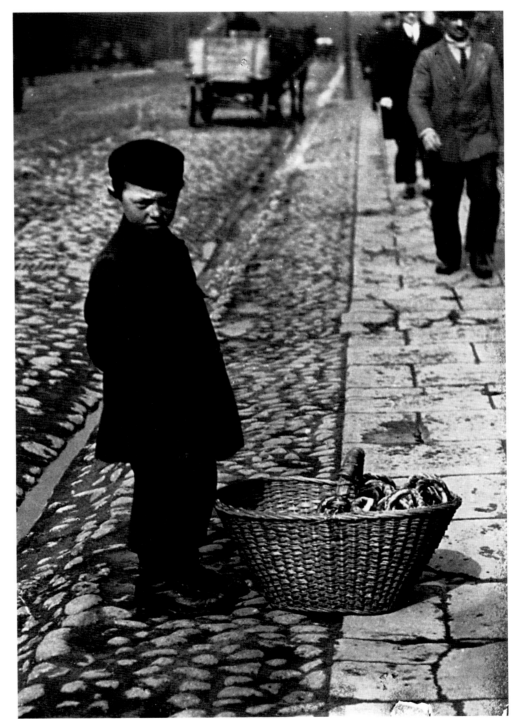

OPPOSITE PAGE

He advertises his wares on his head.

Varshe (Warsaw), 1927

This bagel seller has no permit, so he has to watch
out for the police.

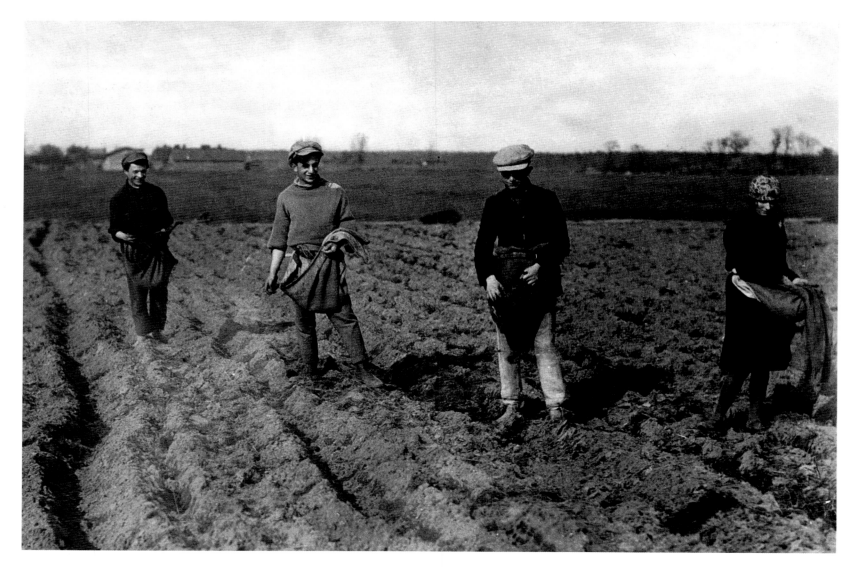

Varshe (Warsaw), 1927

Eretz Israel on the outskirts of Warsaw. *Halutzim* farming in the fields at Grochów.

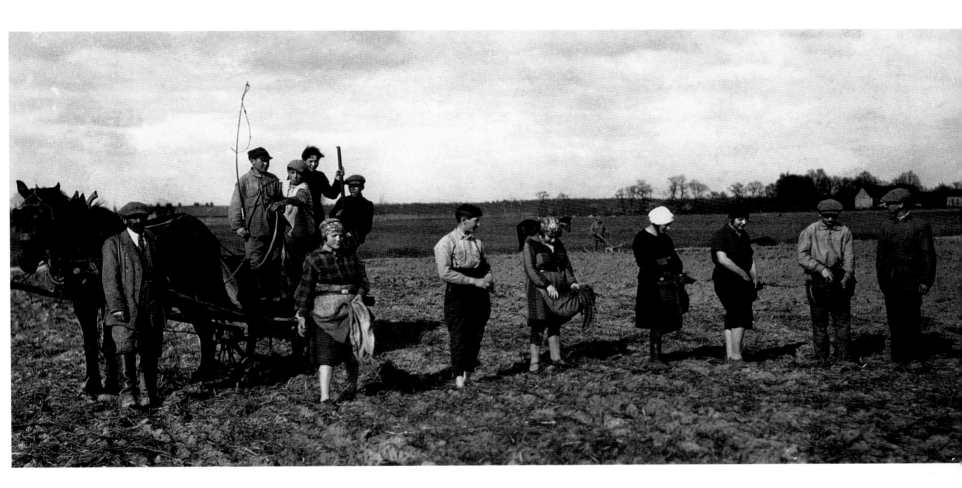

Varshe (Warsaw), 1927

The fields at Grochów

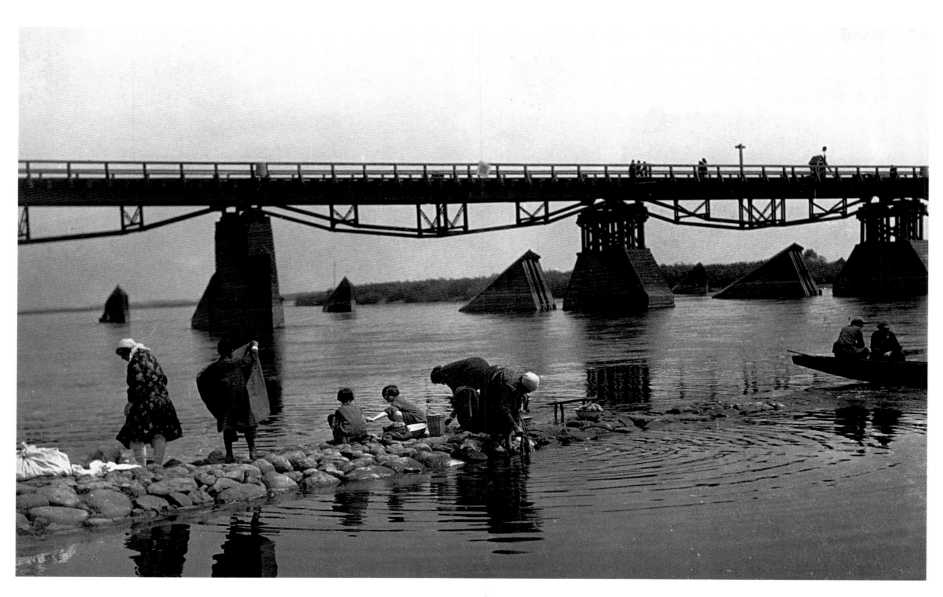

Vishkeve (Wyszków, Warsaw province)

By the bridge

V

AT HOME

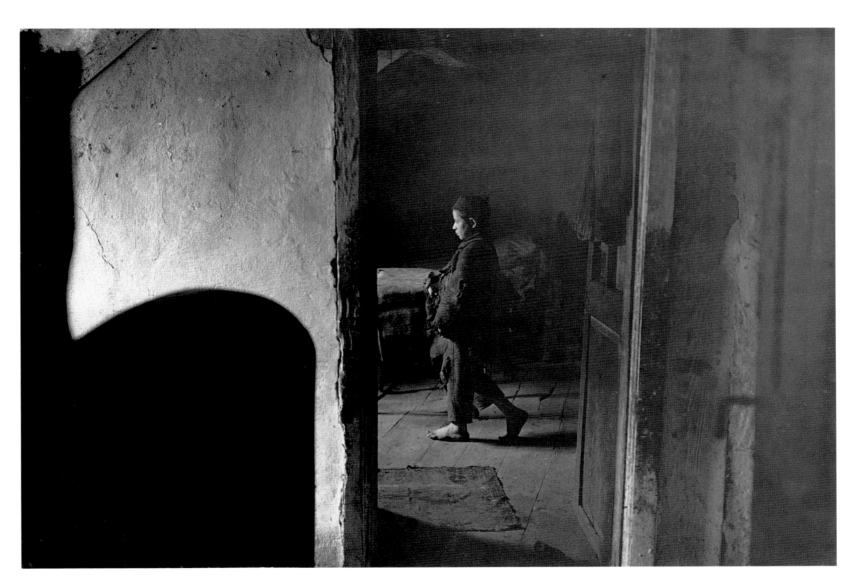

Varshe (Warsaw)

Krochmalna Street

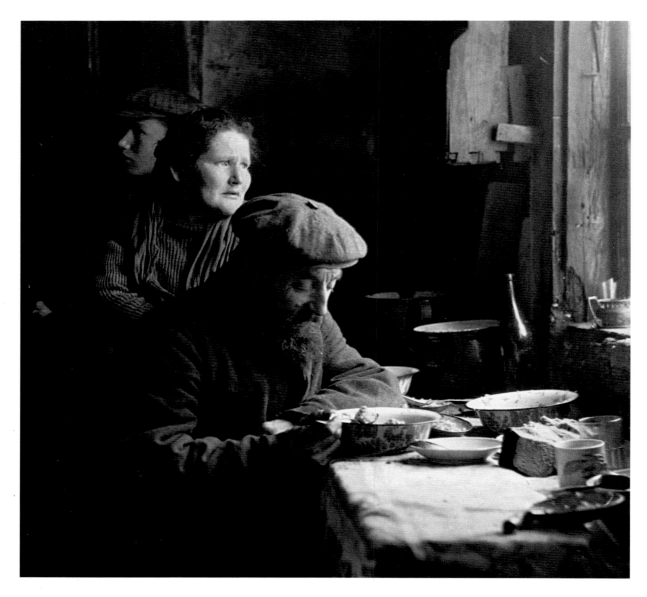

Mezritsh (Międzyrzec, Lublin province), 1924

A laborer's meal

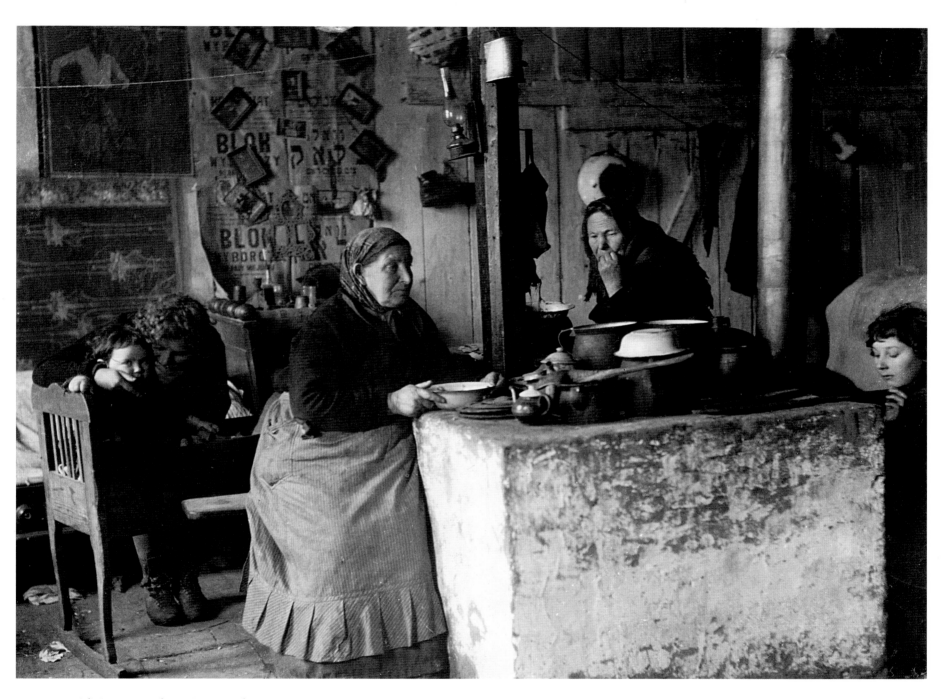

Brisk (Brześć nad Bugiem, Pińsk province)

In the barracks. Five families live in this room.

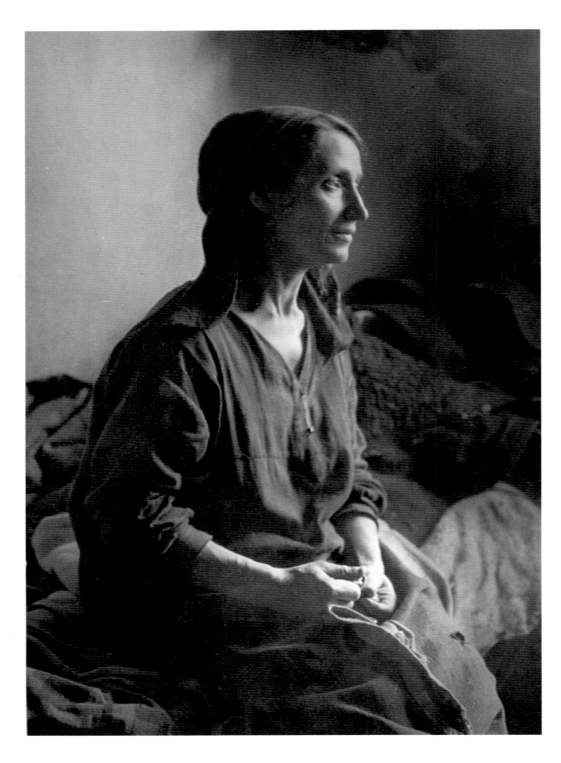

Vishkeve (Wyszków, Warsaw province), 1927
A working woman

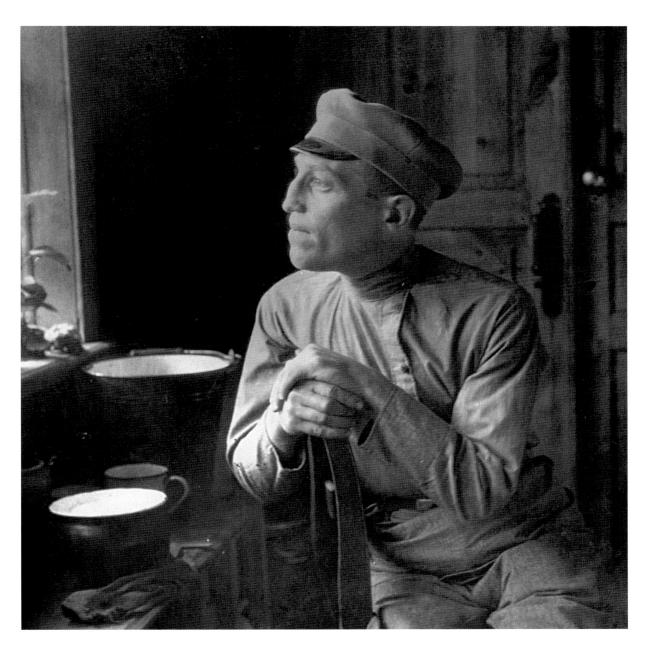

Wilejka (Wilno province), 1927
    A young man from the Russian-Polish border

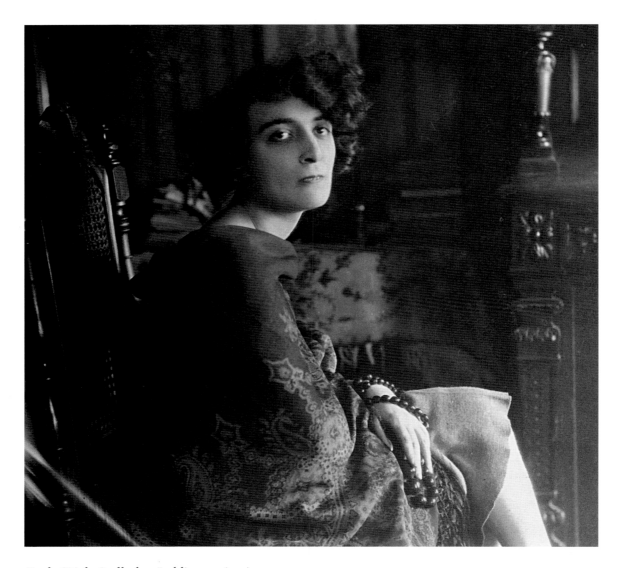

Byale (Biała Podlaska, Lublin province)
　Miss Rabinowicz, the Byaler rebbe's daughter

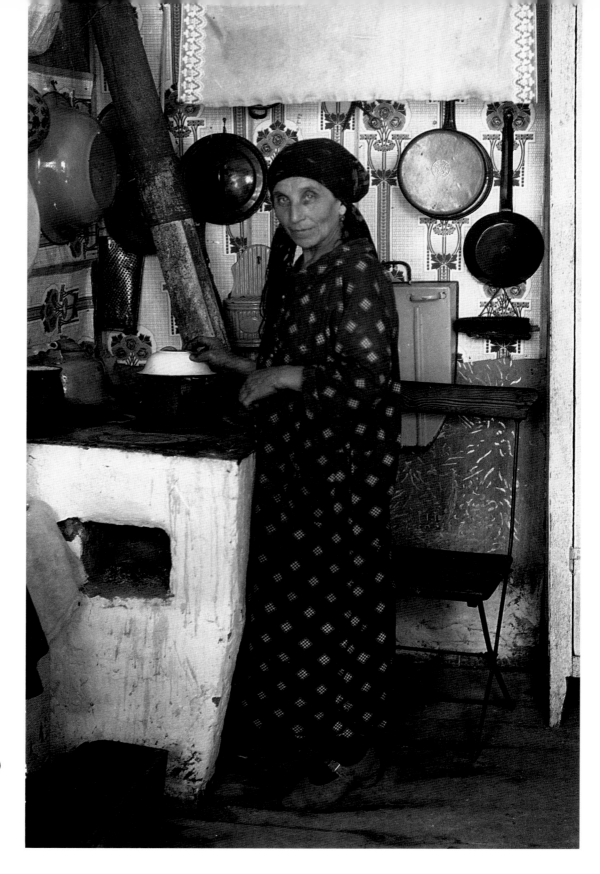

Wołomin (Warsaw province)
The saddler's wife

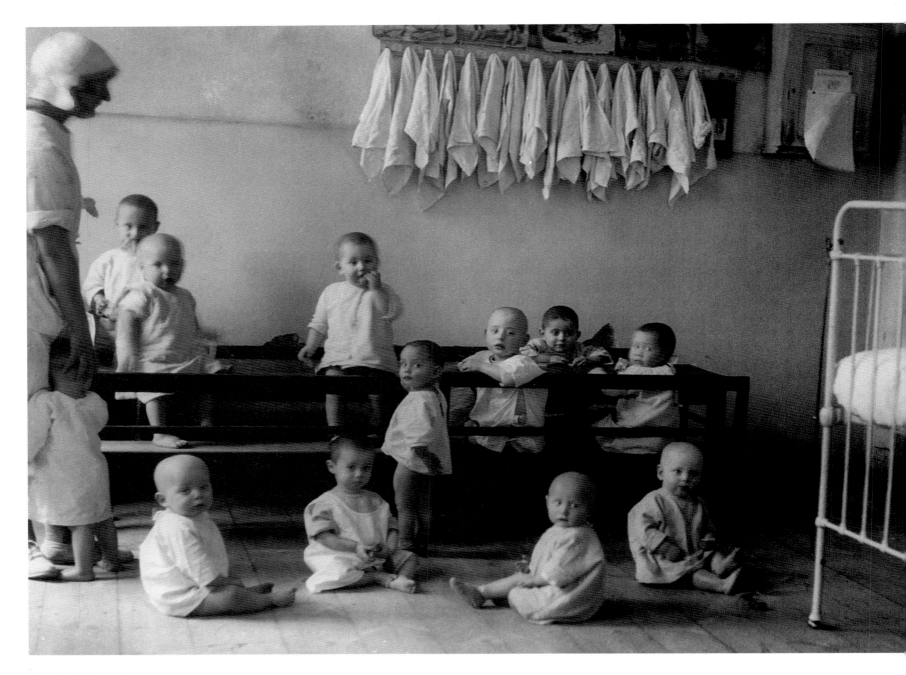

Varshe (Warsaw)

The Jewish home for foundlings

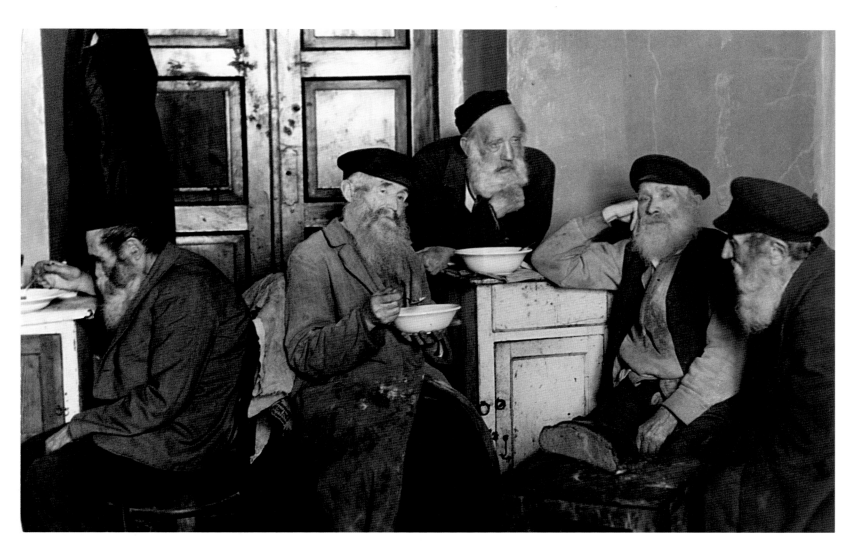

Równe, 1925

In the old-age home

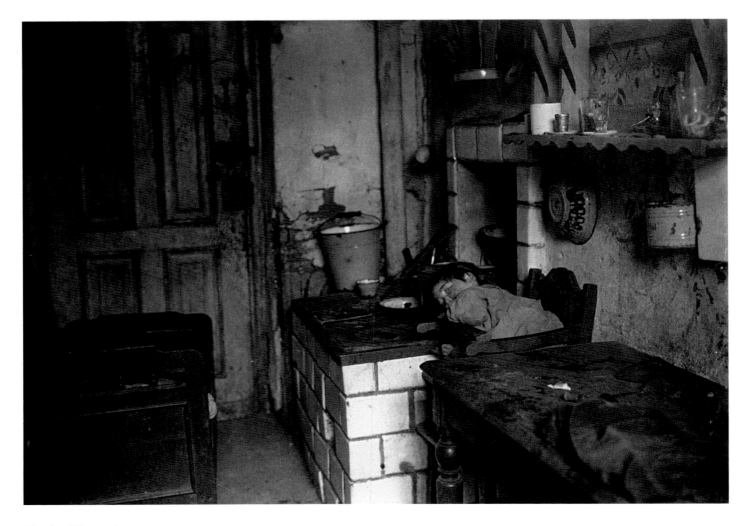

Varshe (Warsaw)

Poverty on Gęsia Street

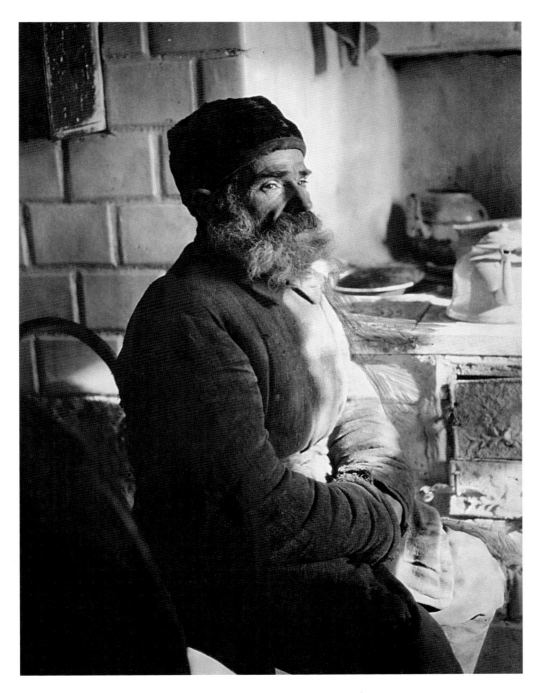

Kosów Lacki (Lublin province), 1928
  Aron Bandrownik, the porter

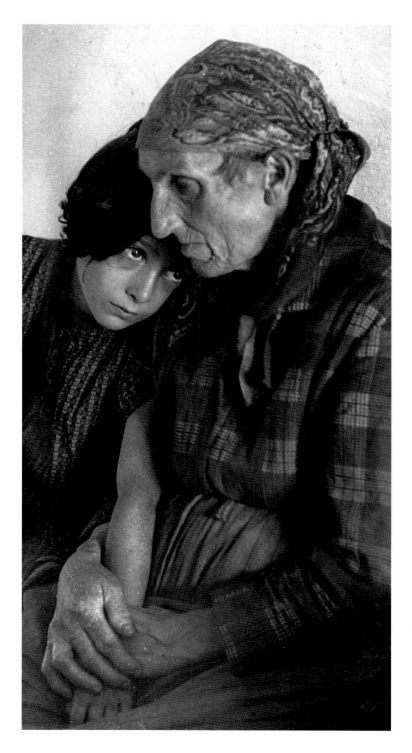

Kurtshev (Karczew, Warsaw province)

Meyer Gurfinkel's wife and granddaughter. Her father is in Washington; her mother is dead.

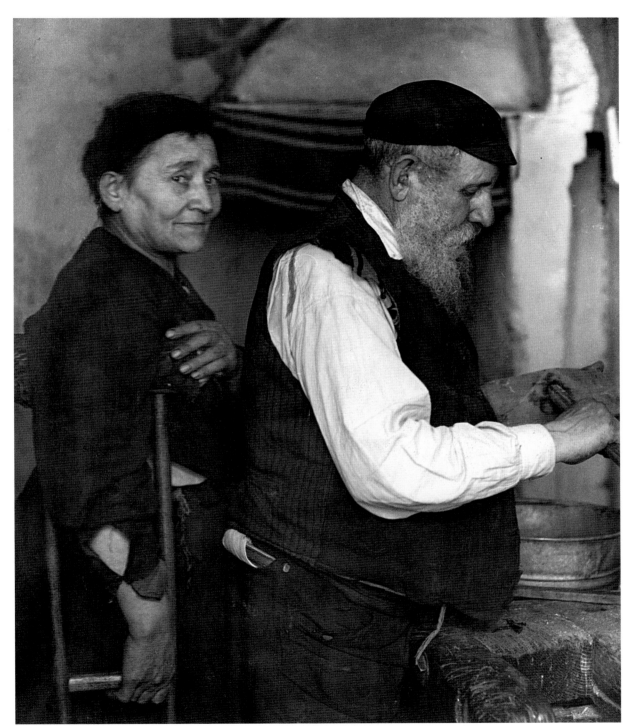

Vishkeve (Wyszków, Warsaw province), 1927

Nokhem, the carpenter, and his wife

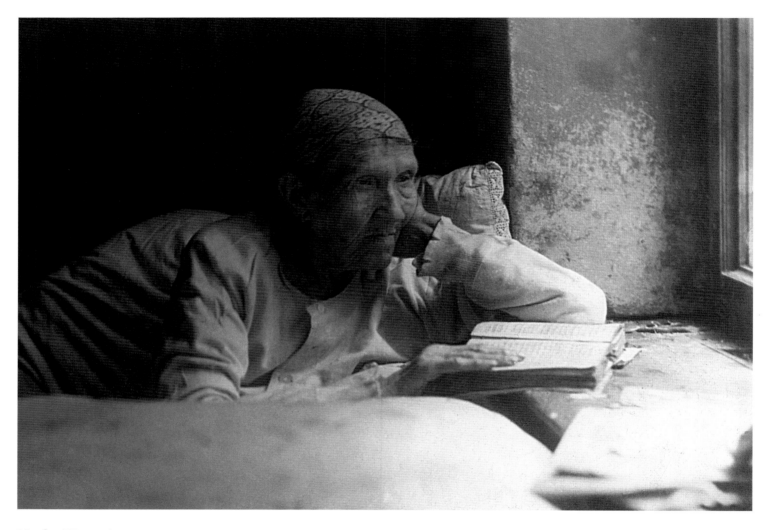

Varshe (Warsaw), 1925

Khane Kolski, one hundred and six years old. Every evening she says *vidui* [a confession of sins] and eats a cookie. Her eighty-year-old son in America does not believe that his mother is still alive.

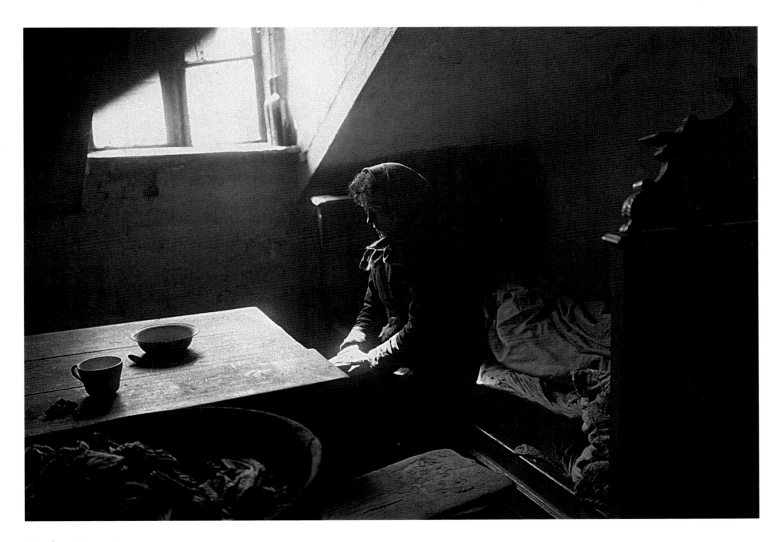

Varshe (Warsaw)
    Krochmalna Street

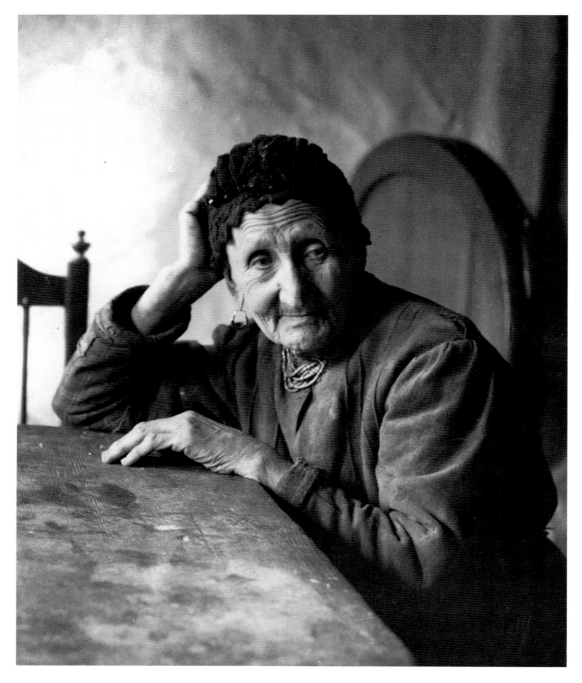

Vishkeve (Wyszków, Warsaw province), 1927
    Itke the glazier's wife, eighty years old

VI

SIMPLE
PLEASURES

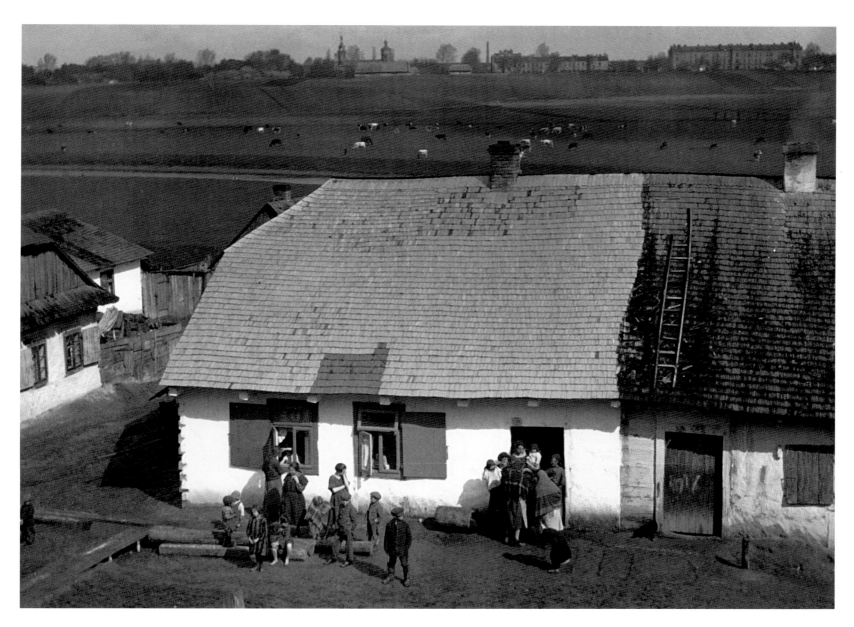

Tshortkev (Czortków, Tarnopol province)

With the Weiners, at the foot of the hill

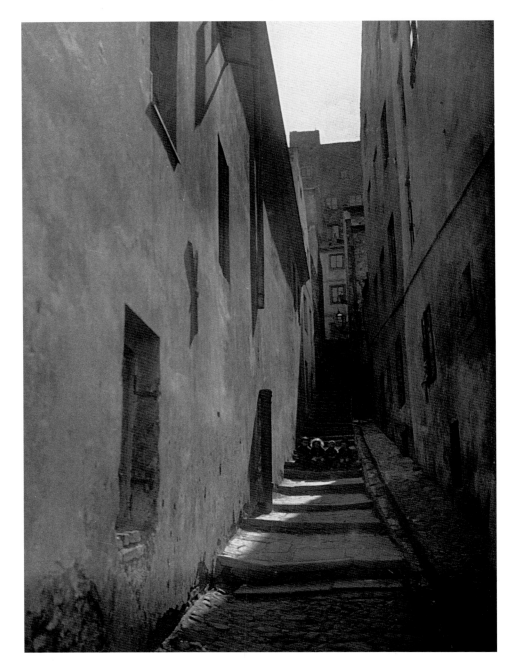

Varshe (Warsaw), the old town

   "Once this was the heart of Warsaw, this labyrinth of narrow alleys winding between tall, gray walls." (*Shtarke un shvakhe*)

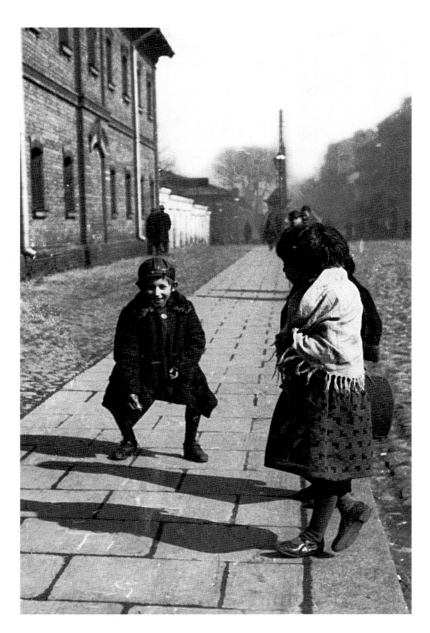

The name of the game is hopscotch.

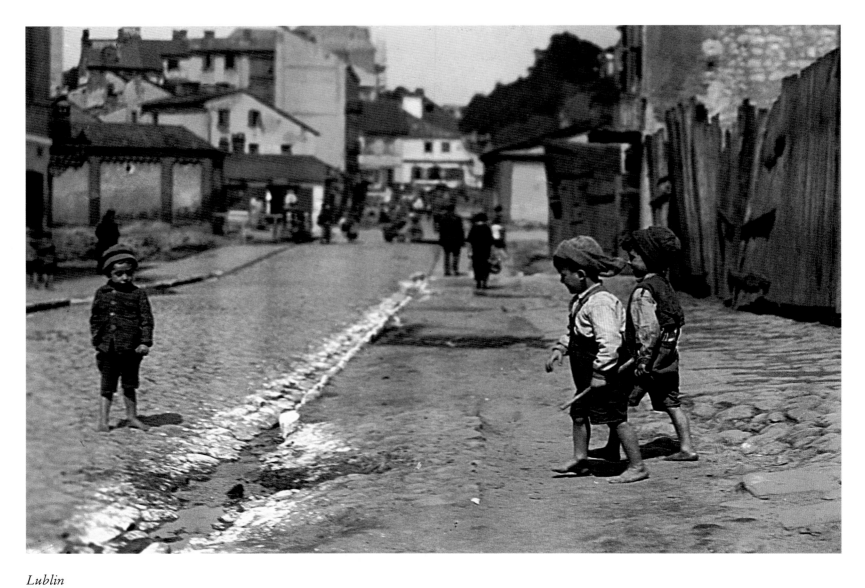

Lublin

The little boy makes it clear which side of the drain is his territory.

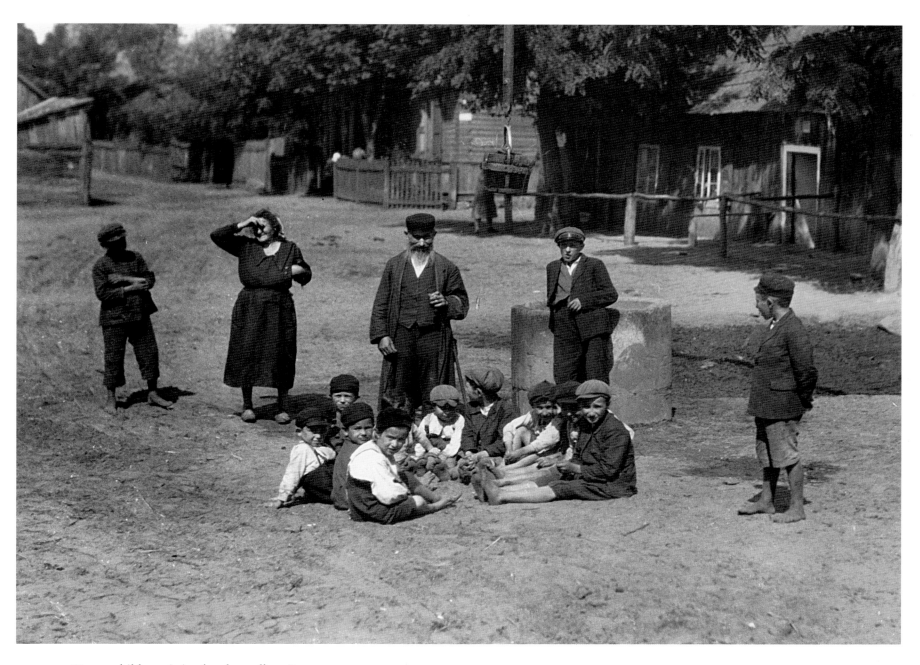

"Seven children sitting by the well . . ."

[From a Yiddish folk song]

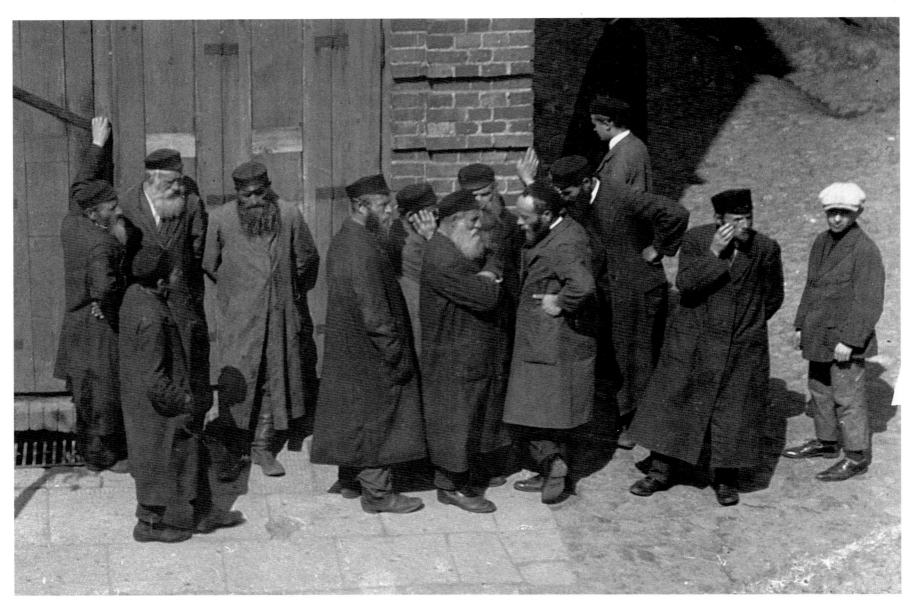

Likeve (Łuków, Lublin province), 1926

A dispute

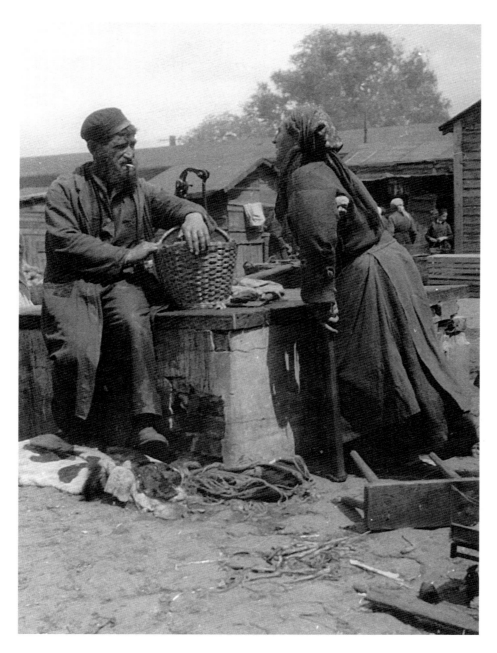

Words are flying

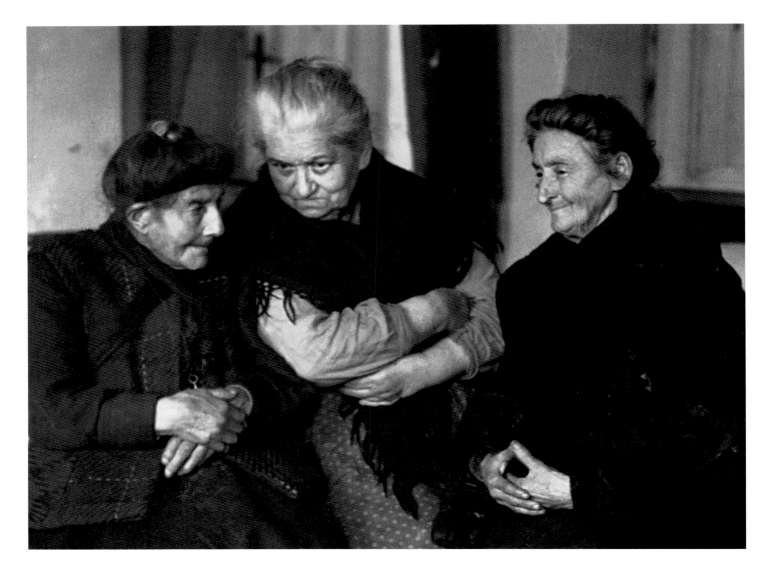

1927

You can learn the latest gossip here.

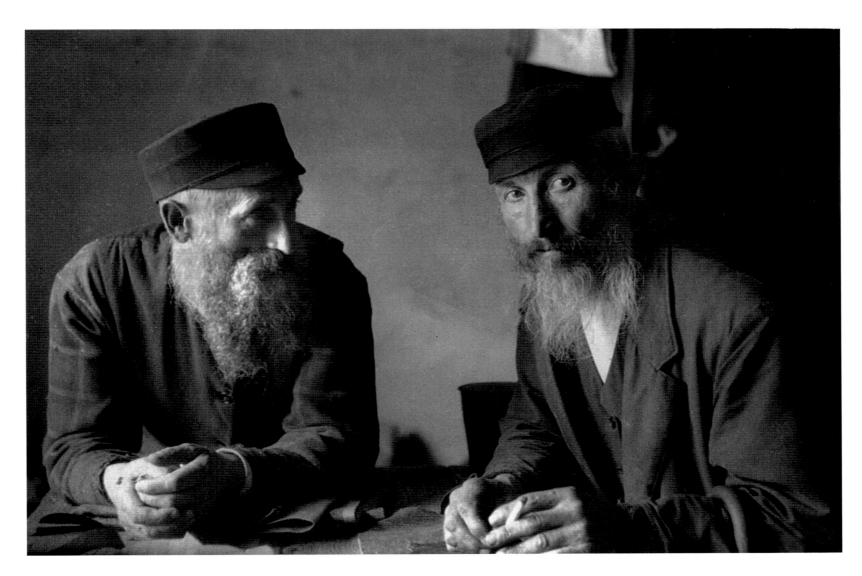

Kurtshev (Karczew, Warsaw province), 1927

A tailor pays a tailor a visit.

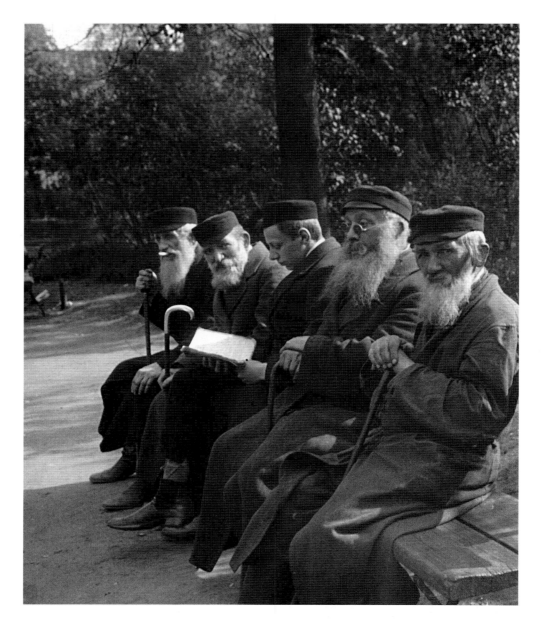

Varshe (Warsaw), 1925

    In the Krasiński gardens: the Jews from Nalewki Street

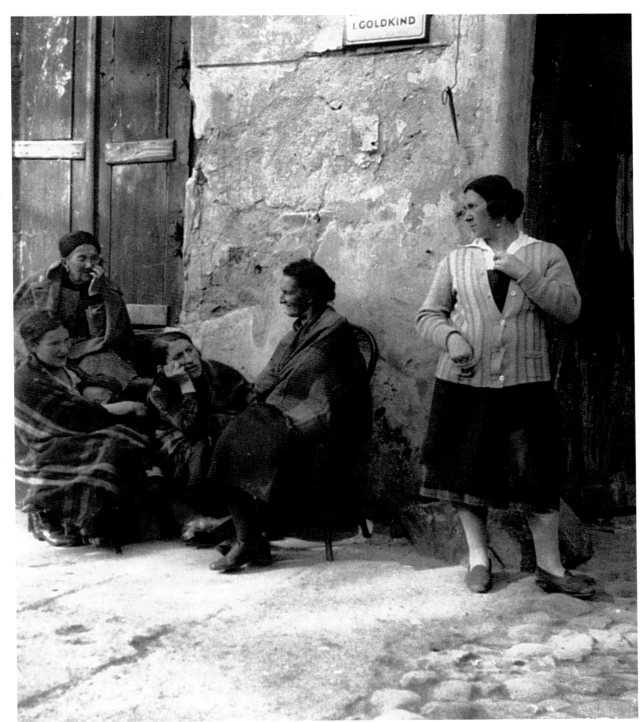

Płock (Warsaw province)

Oyneg shabes

[An *oyneg shabes*—here used ironically—is in fact a traditional Sabbath afternoon gathering for discussion, lectures, and sociability. Literally it means "joy of the Sabbath."]

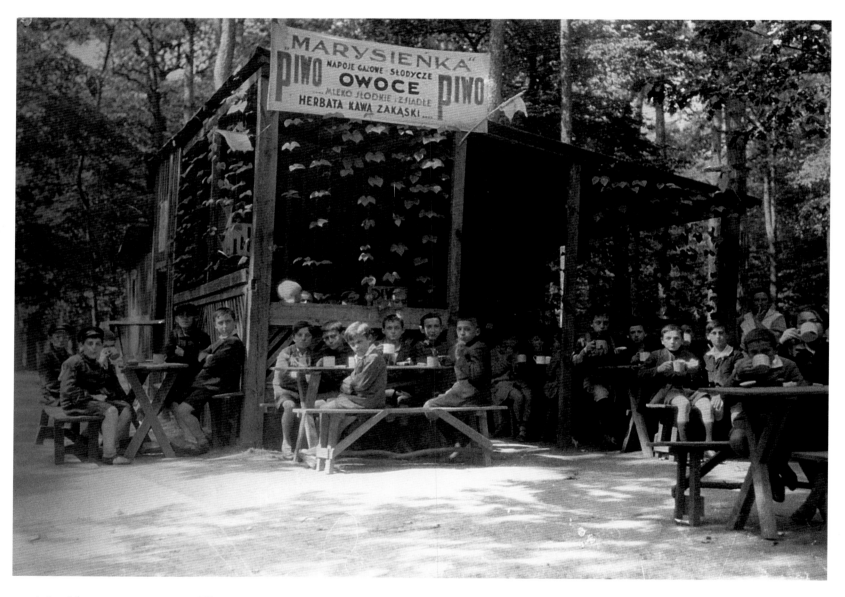

A Jewish summer camp near Warsaw

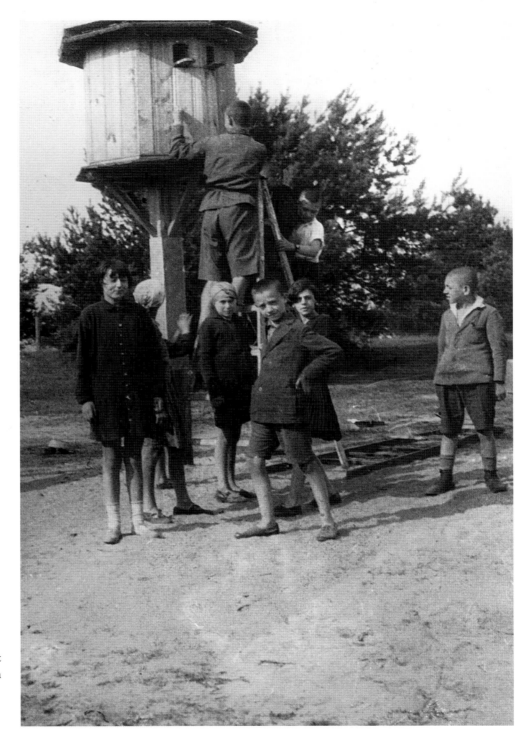

Miedzeszyn (Warsaw province)

Building a bird house in the Medem Sanatorium

[The Medem Children's Sanatorium was a Bundist institution that catered mainly to tubercular children from Jewish working families.]

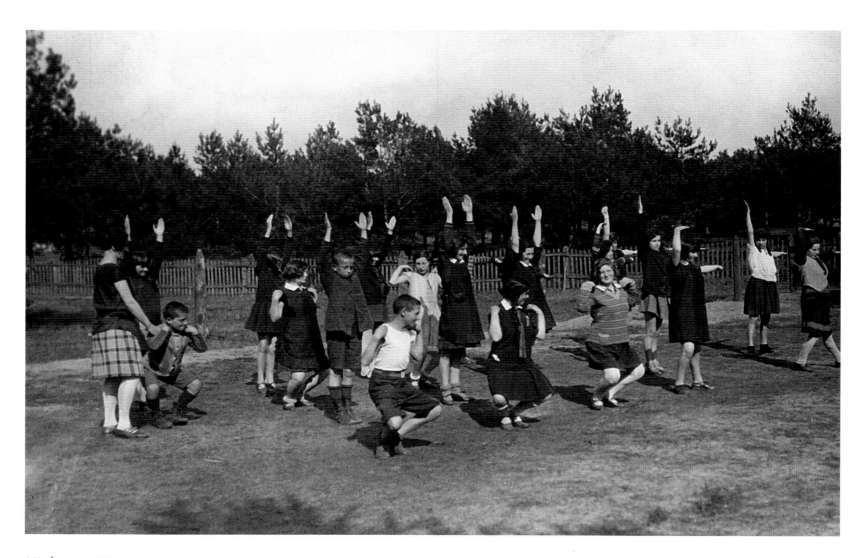

Miedzeszyn (Warsaw province)
  Calisthenics in the Medem Sanatorium

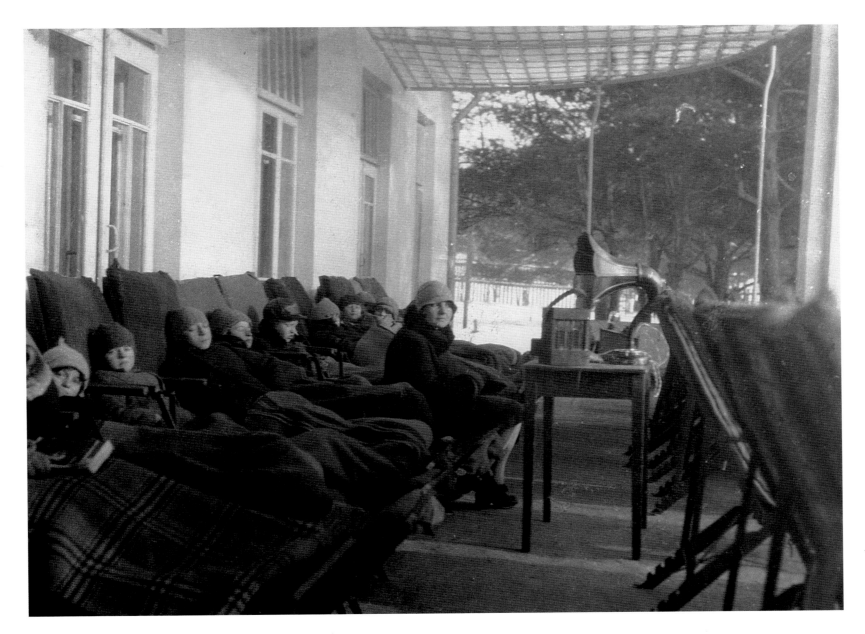

Miedzeszyn (Warsaw province)
   Listening to the radio in the Medem Sanatorium

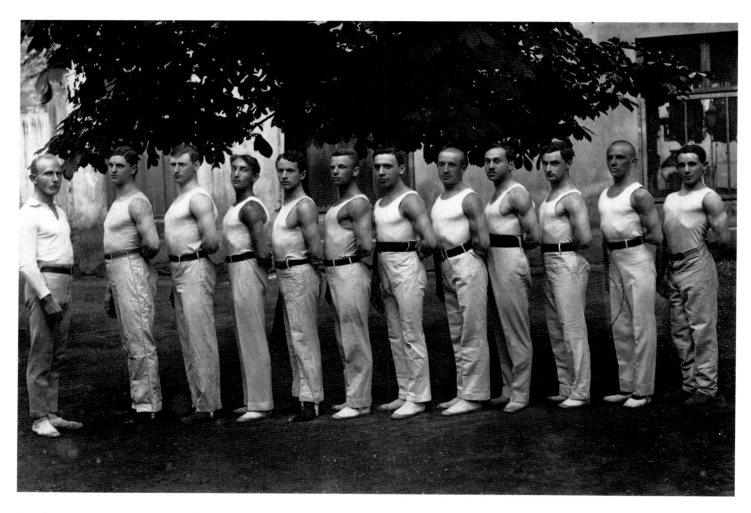

Varshe (Warsaw)

A sports club

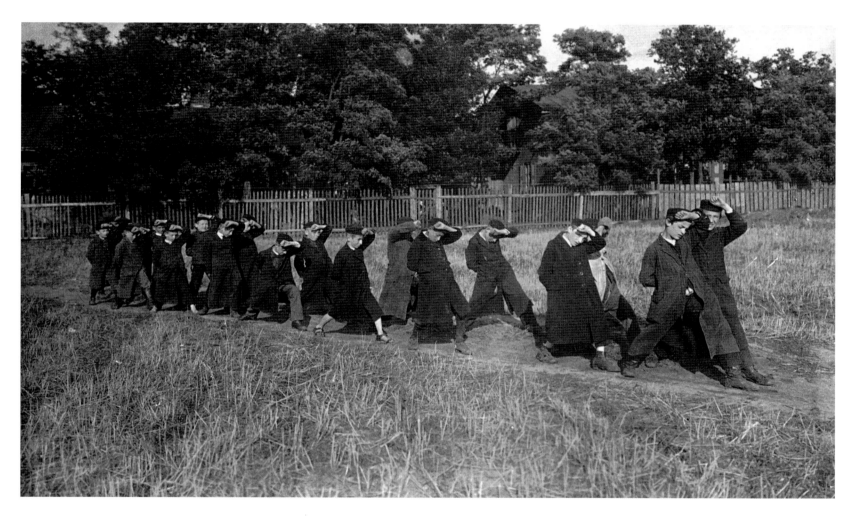

A Mizrachi summer camp

Boys doing excerises in their *kapotes*

[Mizrachi is a religious Zionist movement.]

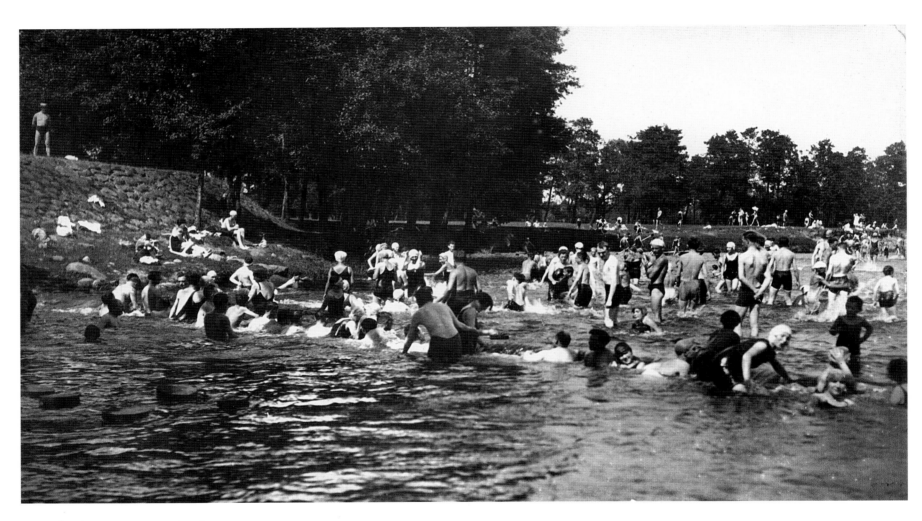

Świder (Warsaw province)

The Świder river on a Saturday

VII

PIETY

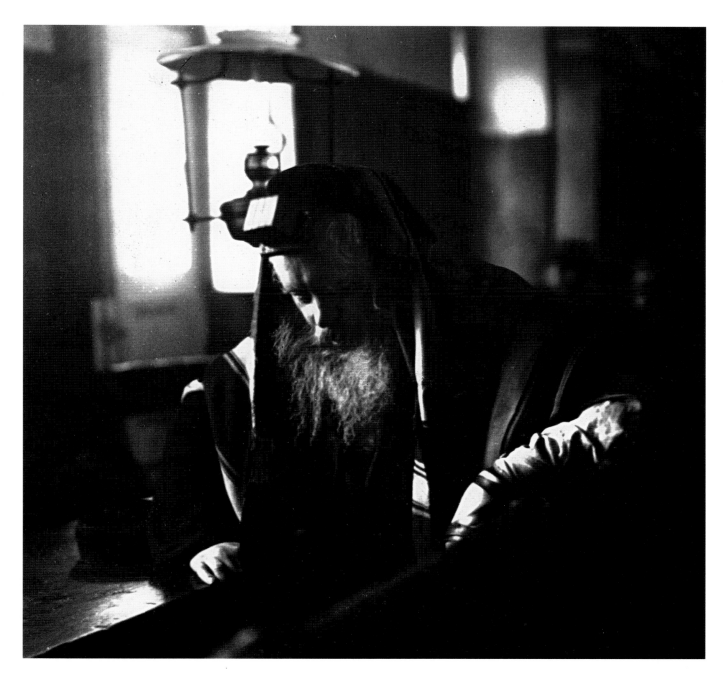

Lublin

He prays

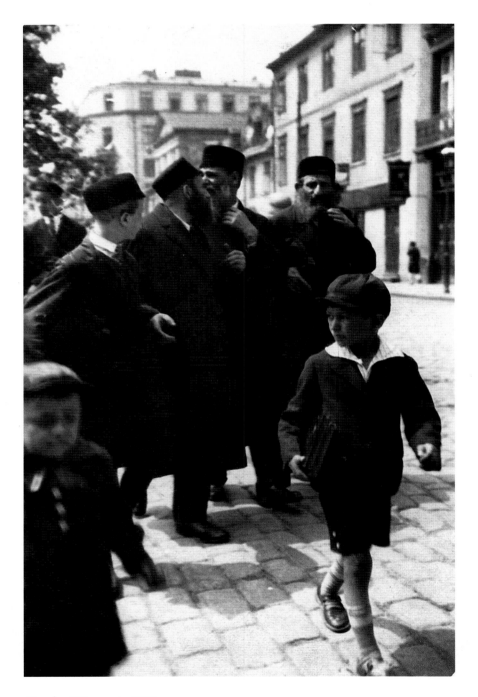

Varshe (Warsaw), 1929

On the way to synagogue

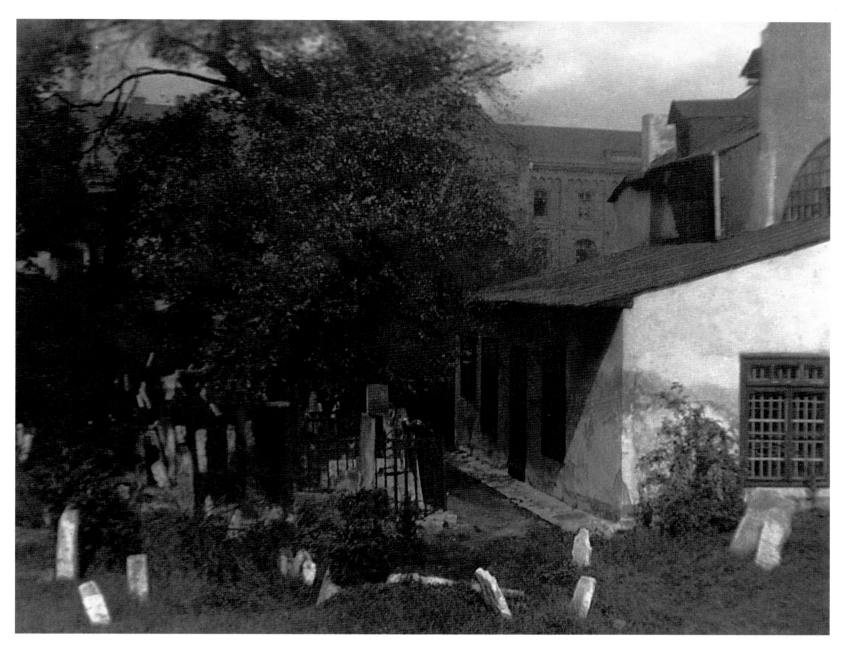

Kroke (Kraków)

The Rema's grave at his synagogue

["Rema" is an acronym for Rabbi Moses Isserles, ca. 1525–1572,
a Talmudic scholar and halakhic authority.]

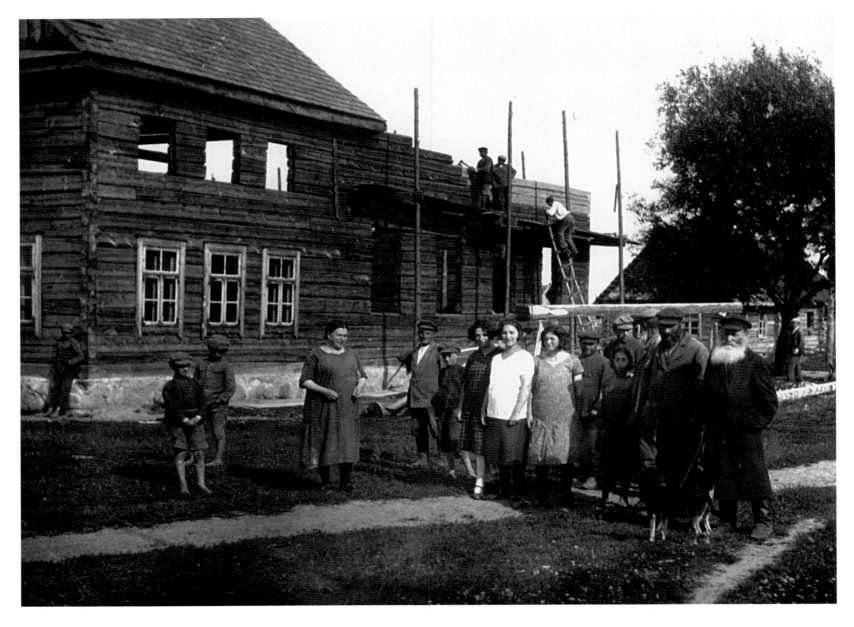

Building a new synagogue

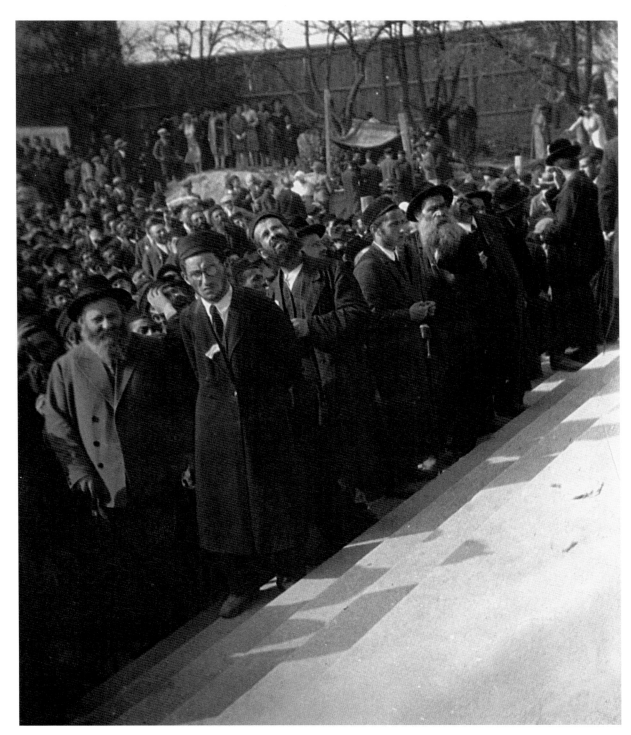

Lublin, 1925

Consecrating the Yeshiva
Hakhmei Lublin

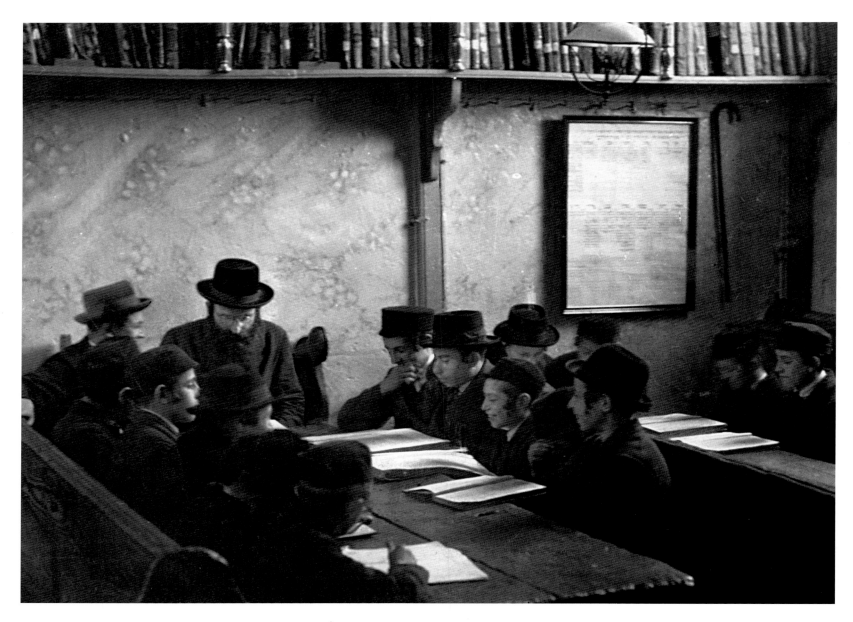

Rayshe (Rzeszów, Lwów province)
   In the Raysher yeshiva

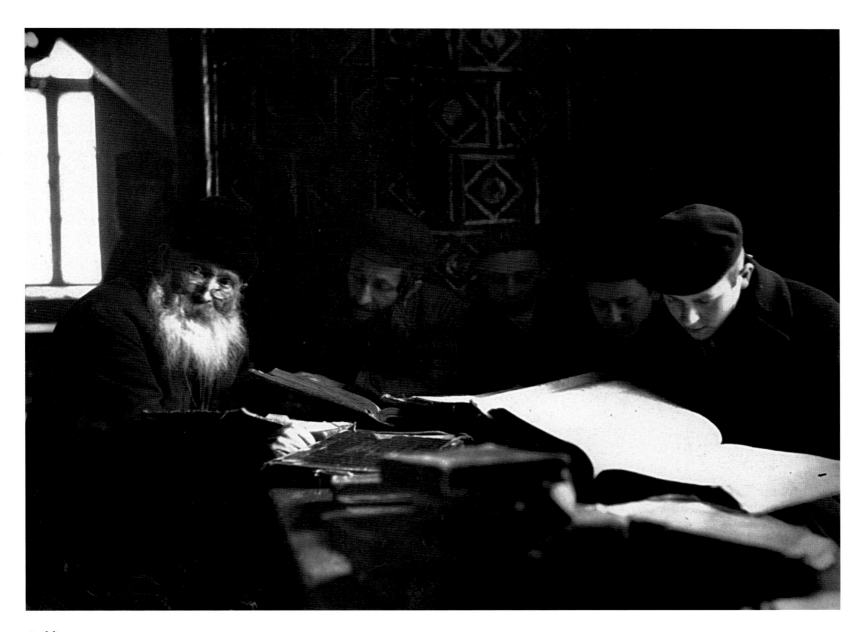

Lublin

The young and the old study together

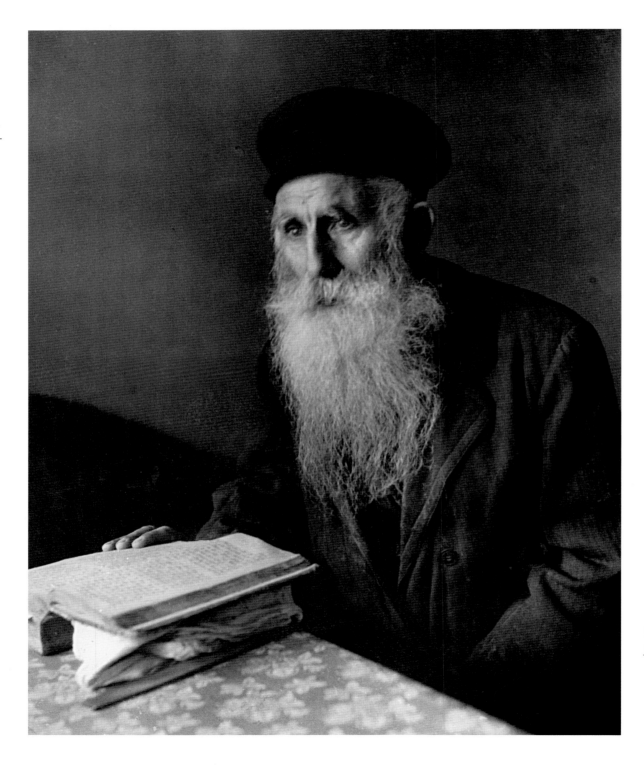

Visoke Litovsk (Wysokie Litewskie, Pińsk province), 1927

The synagogue beadle for forty years, Moishe Pinchuk is a sweet man, a town favorite.

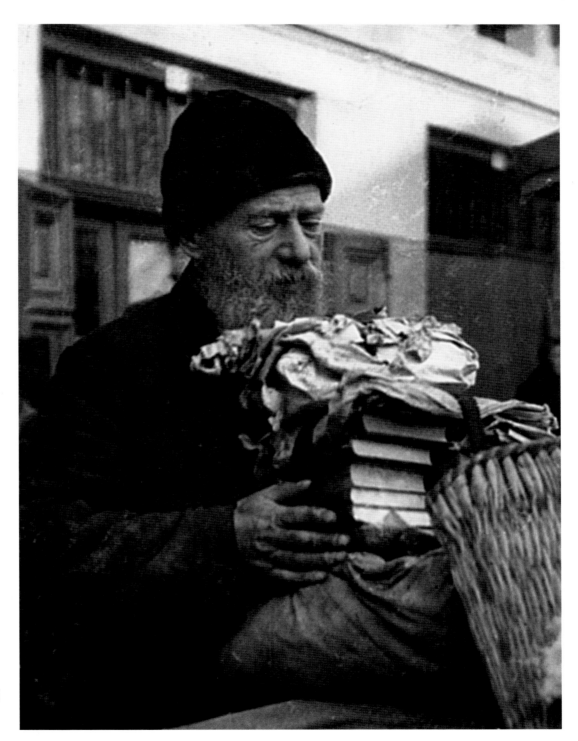

Siddurim for sale

[The siddur is the daily prayer book.]

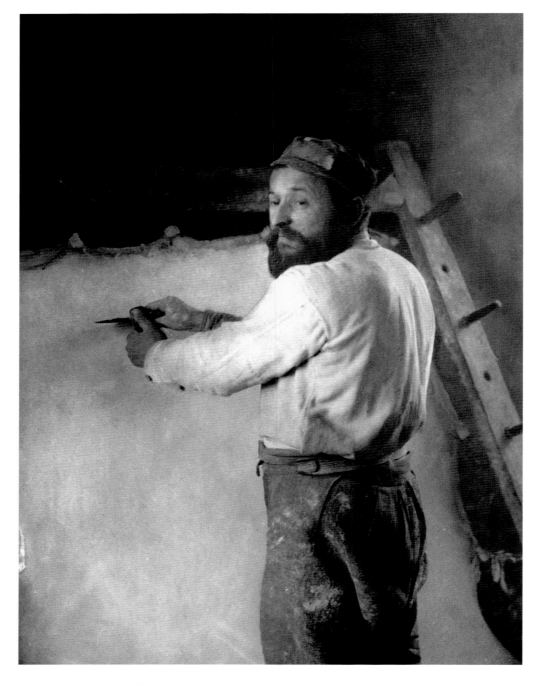

Likeve (Łuków, Lublin province), 1926
Making parchment for Torah scrolls

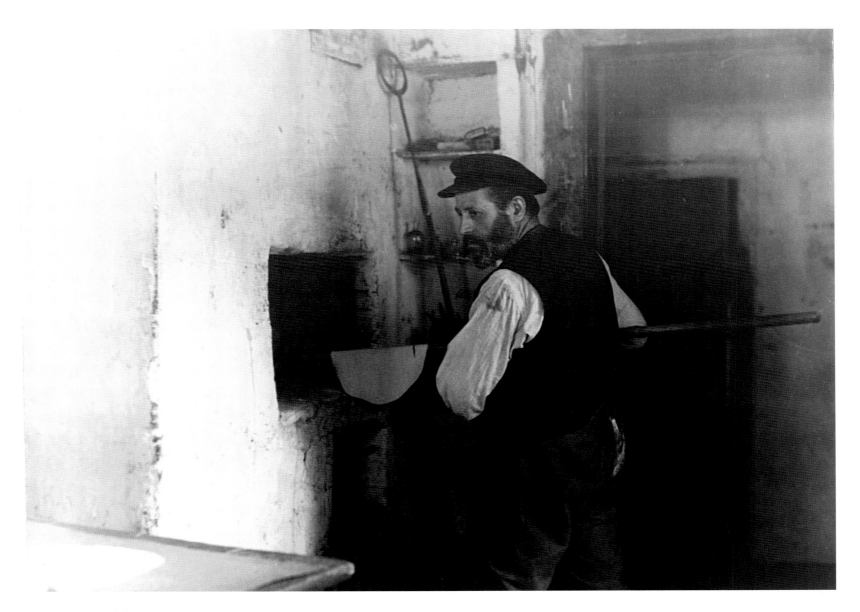

Lida (Nowogródek province), 1926

His matzohs are shipped as far as Warsaw.

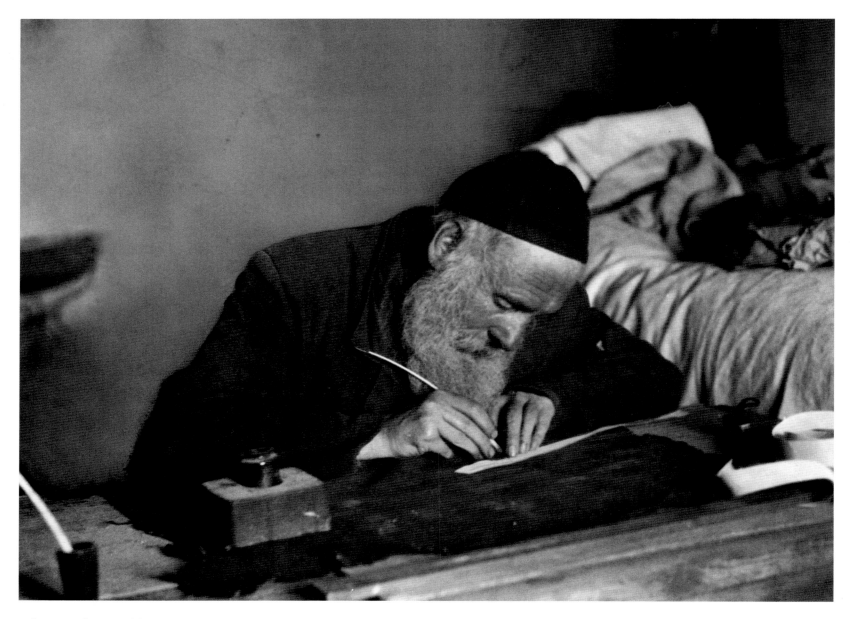

Likeve (Łuków, Lublin province), 1926
  Moishe-Yankev, the oldest scribe in Łuków

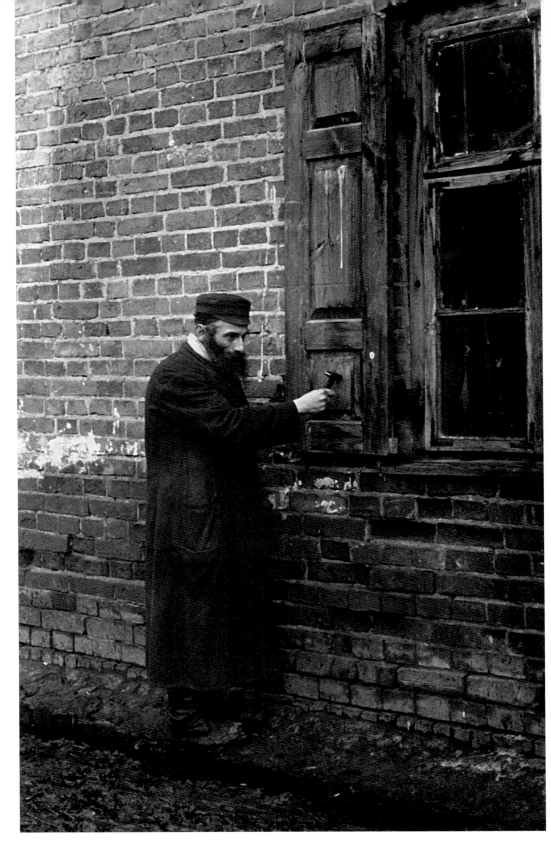

Byale (Biała Podlaska, Lublin province), 1926

Azrielke, the *Shabes-klaper*. On Friday evenings he knocks on the shutters, announcing the beginning of the Sabbath.

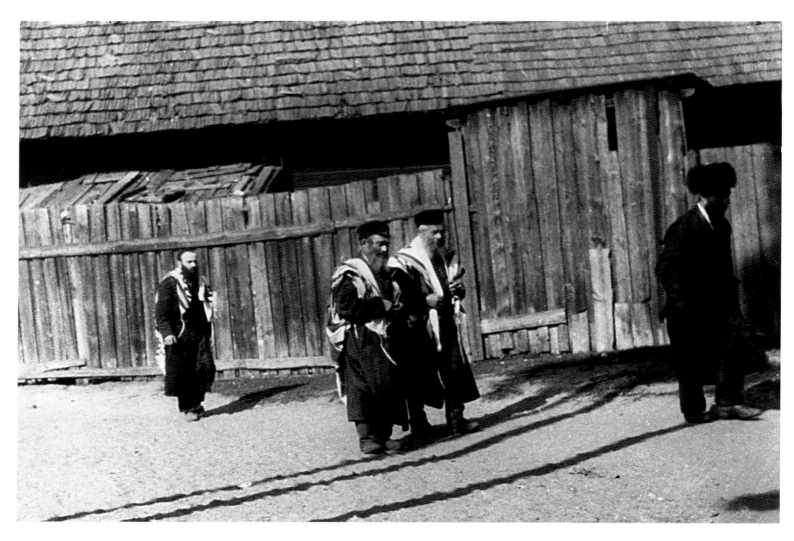

Otwock (Warsaw province)

The hasidim are on their way to the rebbe's house to make Kiddush for the holiday.

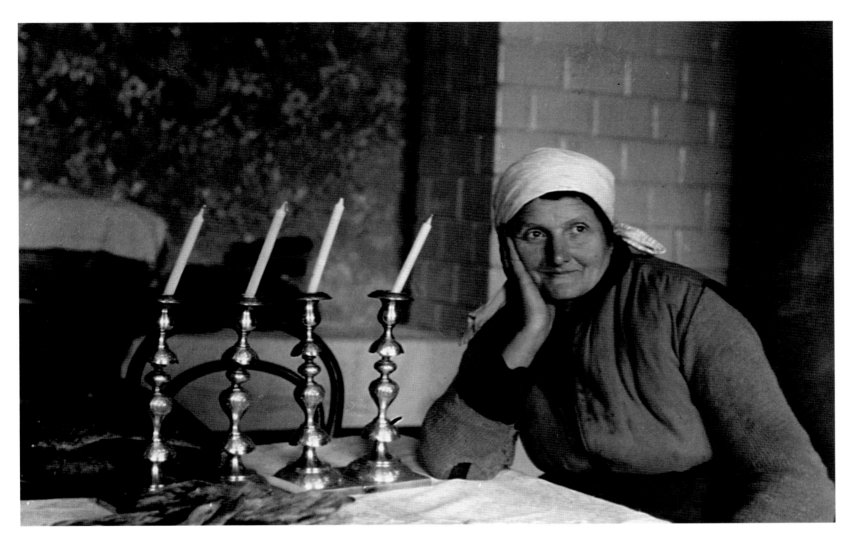

Ger (Góra Kalwaria, Warsaw province)

The poor man's Sabbath meal is ready. Eydl Karbman at her table.

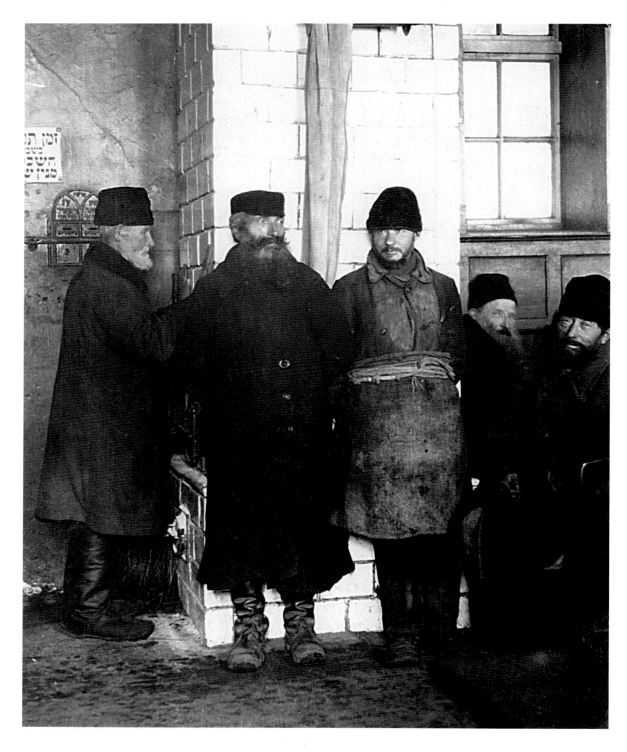

Lublin, 1928

Winter flies: Five city burghers
hug the synagogue stove.

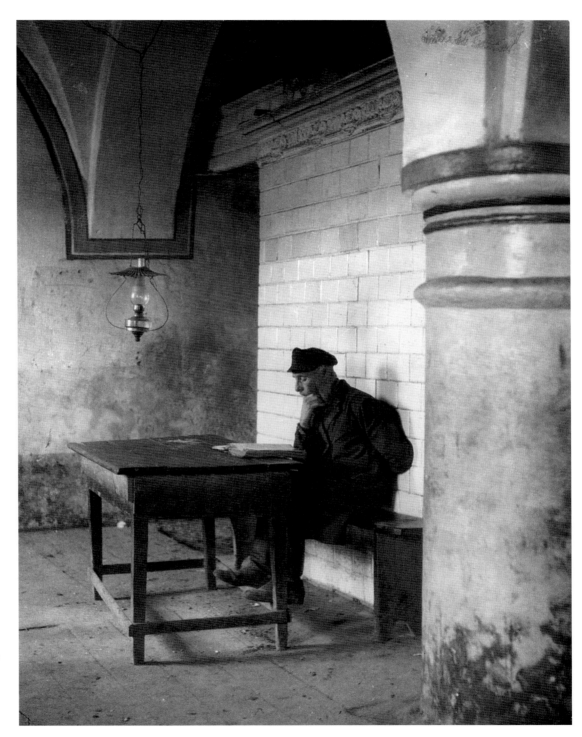

*Visoke Litovsk (Wysokie Litewskie,
Pińsk province)*

In the old synagogue

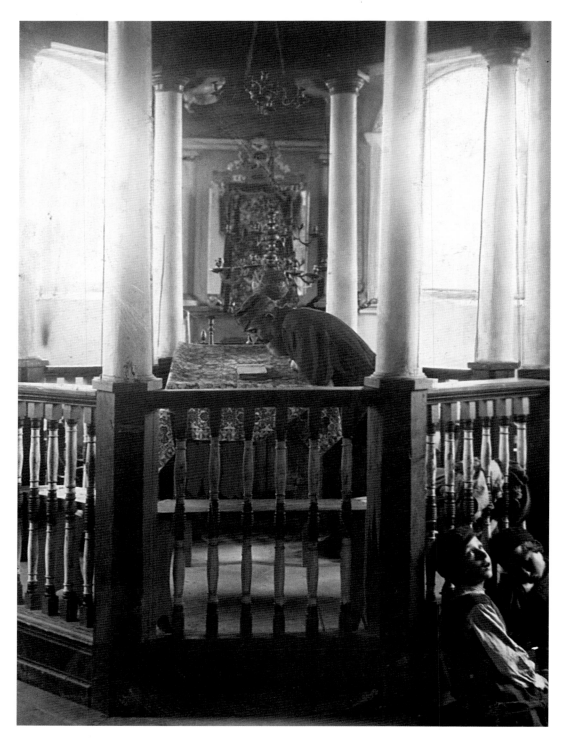

Lublin, 1924

This synagogue on the outskirts of Lublin
goes back to the time of the Tatars.

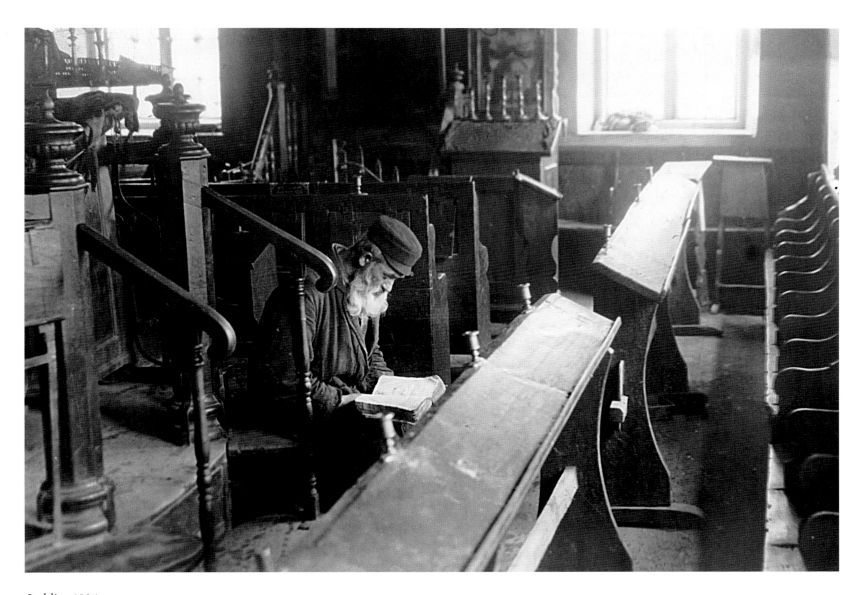

Lublin, 1924

The Saul Wahl Synagogue, the oldest in the city

[Legend has it that in 1587 Saul Wahl, a Jew, was made king of Poland for twenty-four hours.]

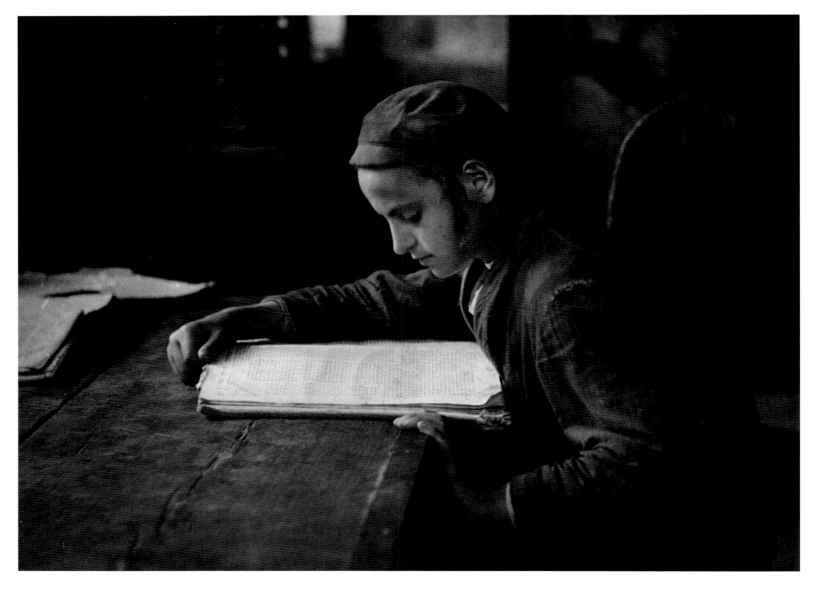

Pyasetshne (Piaseczno, Warsaw province), 1928

A boy studying the Gemara

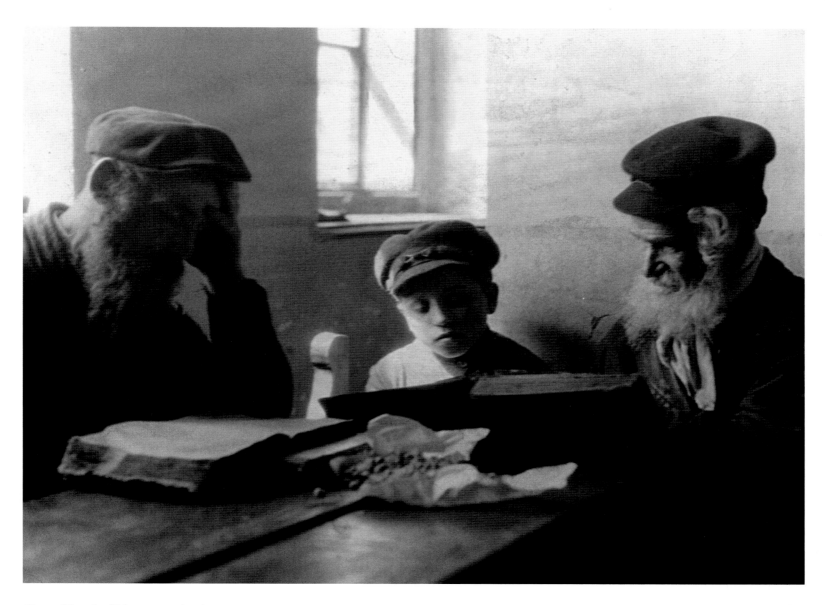

Ostre (Ostróg, Równe province)

Levi the scribe and his two mismatched students

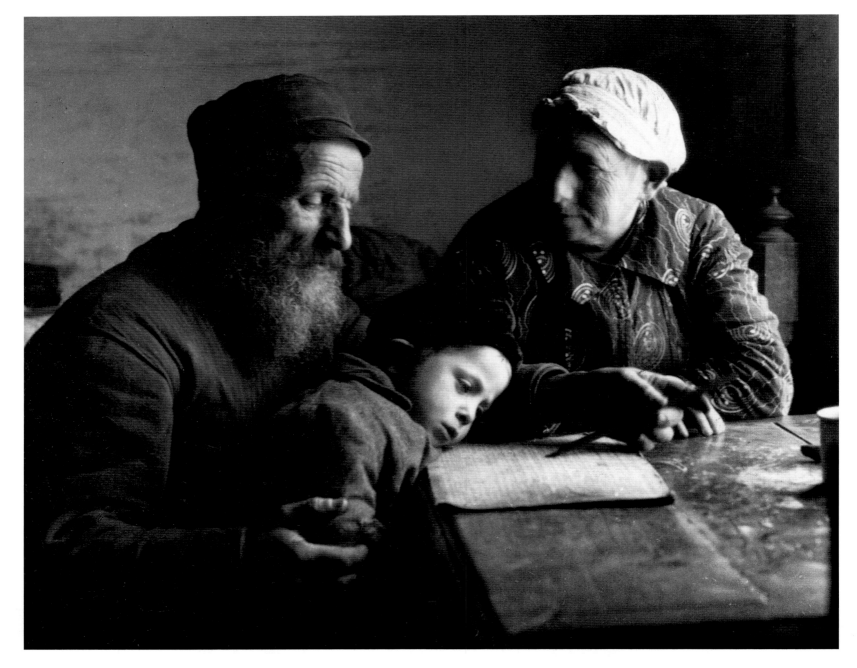

Byale (Biała Podlaska, Lublin province), 1926

Wolf Nachowicz, the gravedigger, teaches his grandson to read while the
boy's grandmother looks on with pleasure. (The father is in America.)

VIII

LEAVING

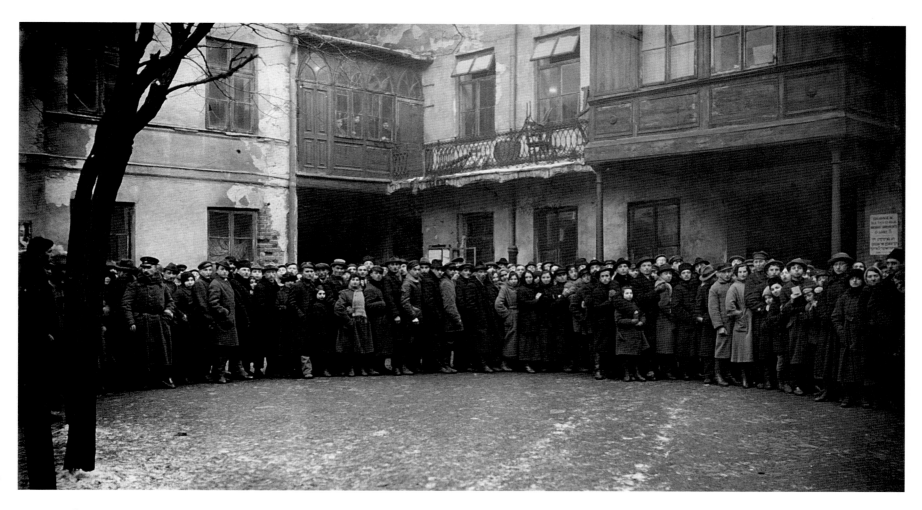

Hebrew Immigrants Aid Society (HIAS) in Warsaw

The snail walk

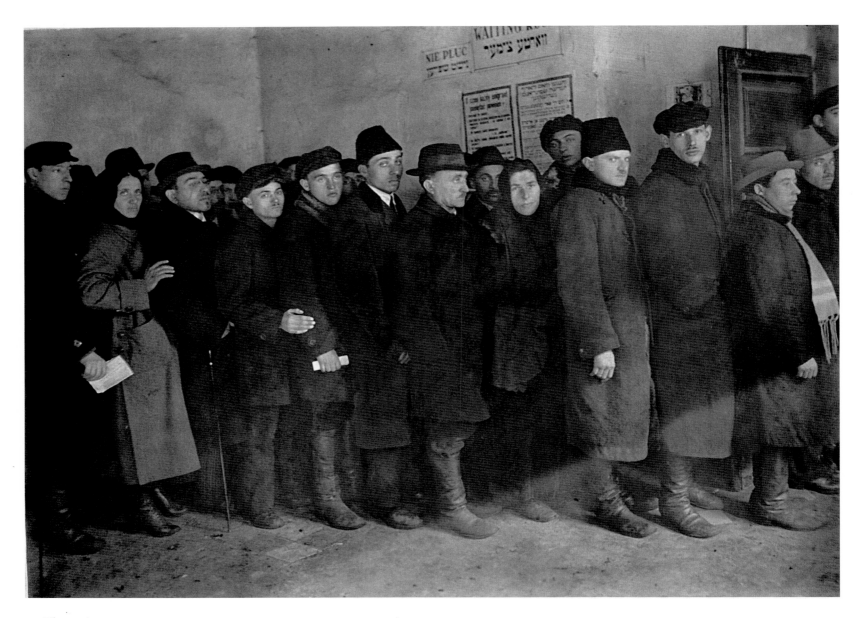

The wait

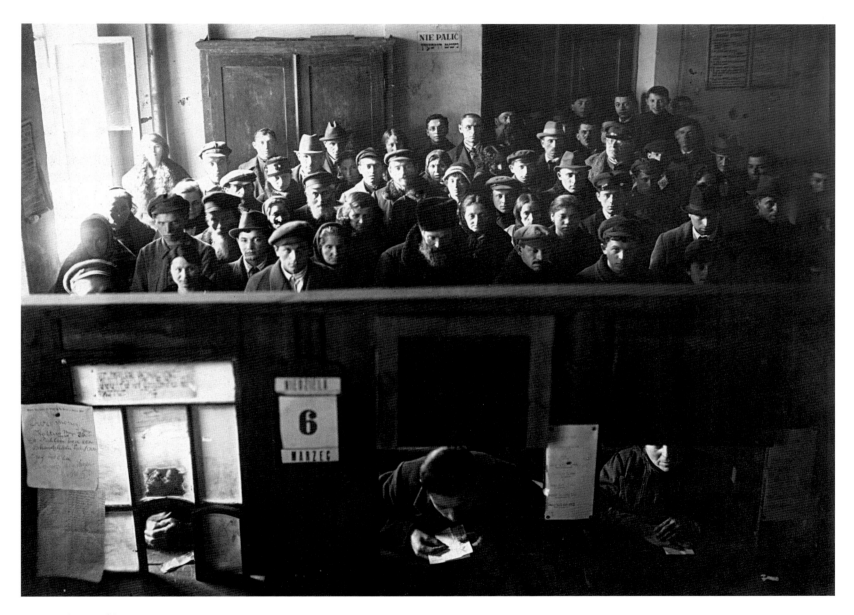

Windows of hope

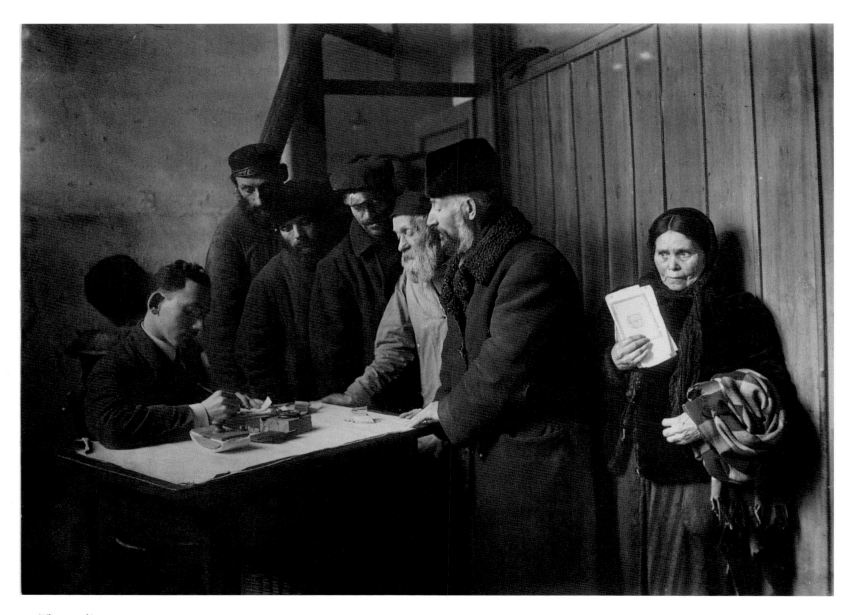

The applicants

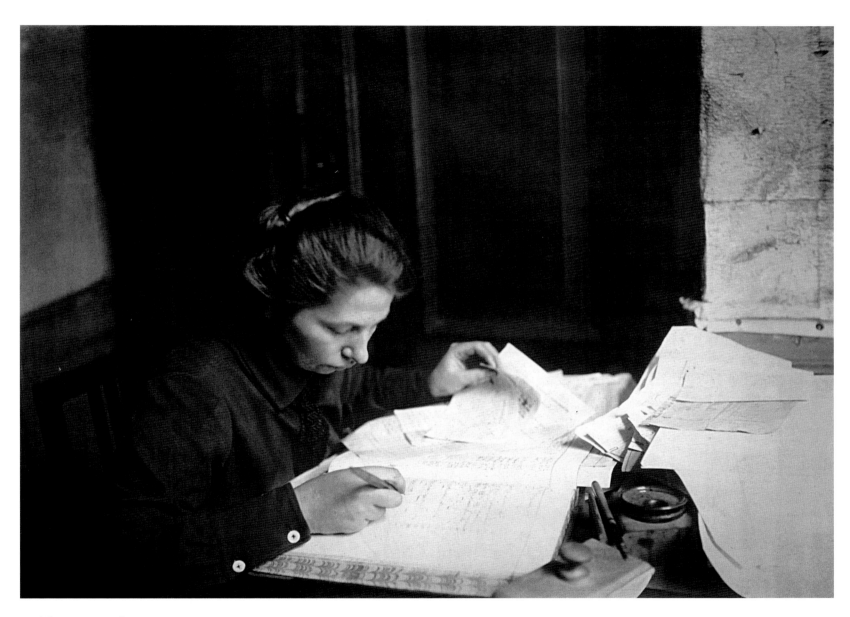

The paperwork

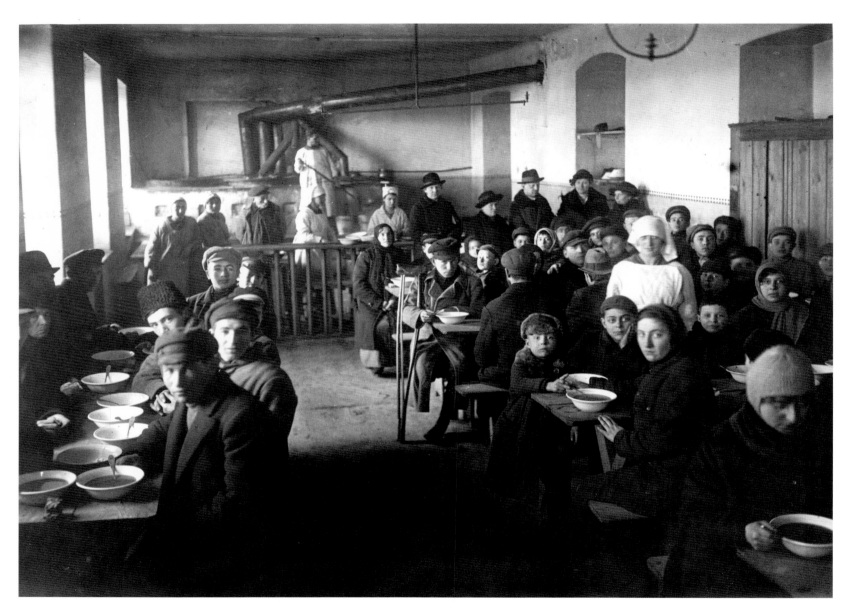

In the HIAS shelter, a shared meal

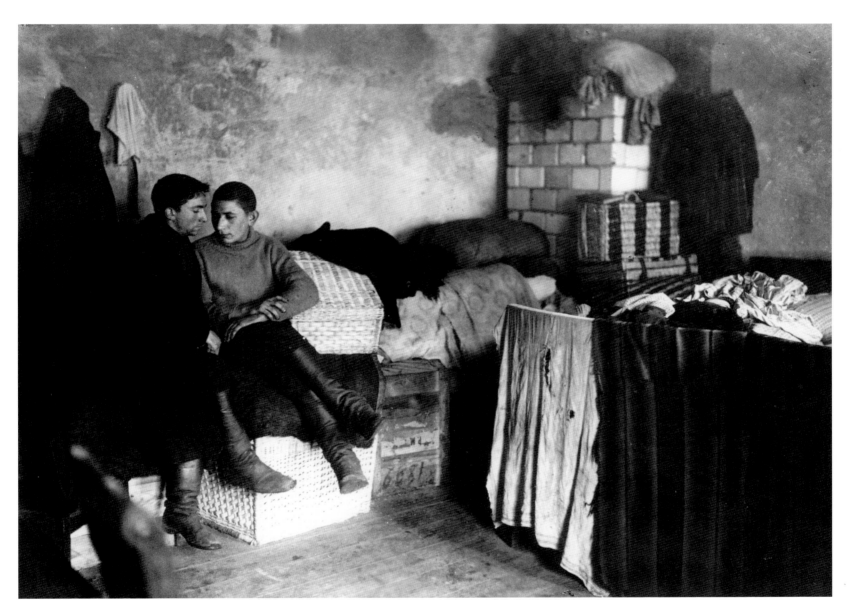

In the shelter, two brothers with all their possessions

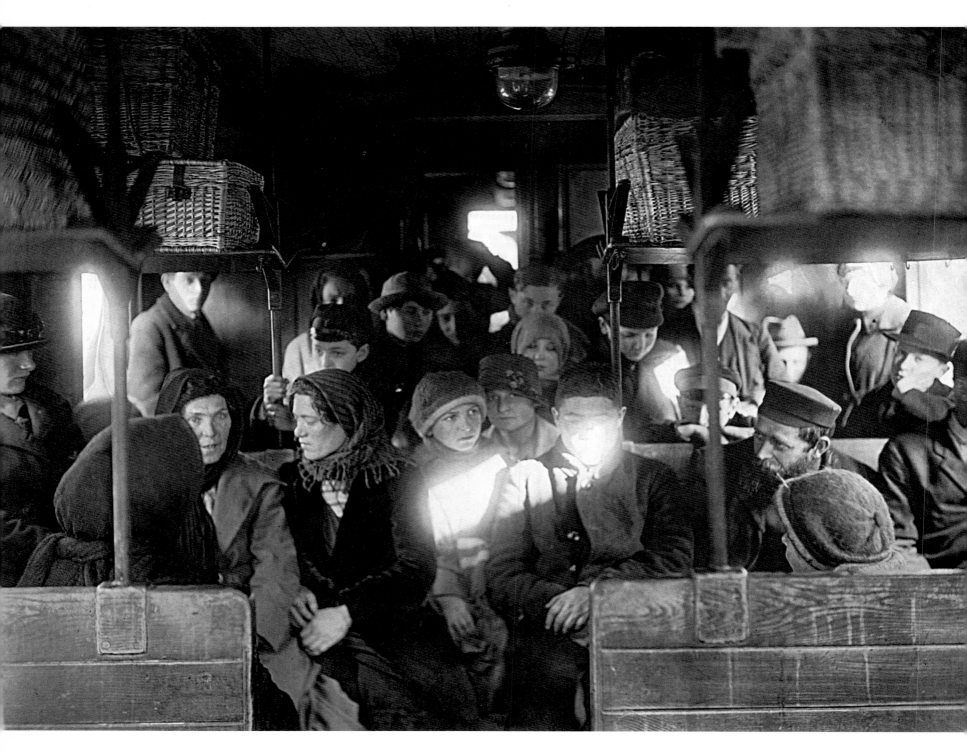

The journey begins: Immigrants on the way to Gdańsk

NOTES

1 Reminiscences about I. L. Peretz in *Di yudishe velt*, April–May 1915.

2 Yitskhok Varshavsky [Isaac Bashevis Singer], "Fun der nayer un alter heym" (From the New and Old Home), *Jewish Daily Forward*, April 10, 1964.

3 Published in the Yiddish literary magazine *Di khalyastre almanakh*, no. 1, Kiev, 1919, and in the book of short stories *Perl* (The Pearls), Warsaw: Kultur-liga, 1922.

4 This quotation and the subsequent ones from Kacyzne's letters to Cahan are excerpted from Papers of Abraham Cahan, YIVO Archives, f.18.

5 Varshavsky, "Fun der nayer un alter heym."

6 Jacob Rotbaum, "Alter Kacyzne—der mentsh un kinstler" (Alter Kacyzne—the man and artist), *Folks-shtime*, Warsaw, April 17, 1982.aa

7 Moshe Dluznowsky, "Drames un baladn fun Alter Kacyzne" (Plays and Ballads of Alter Kacyzne), *Unzer vort*, Paris, January 24, 1970.

8 Nakhman Blitz, "Der kreyts-veg fun Alter Kacyzne" (The Martyrdom of Alter Kacyzne), *Dos naye lebn*, no. 10, Łódź, 1945.